C000175480

KARMA COOKBOOK

GREAT TASTING DISHES TO NOURISH YOUR BODY AND FEED YOUR SOUL

BOY GEORGE
& DRAGANA G. BROWN

CARROLL & BROWN PUBLISHERS LIMITED

First published in 2001 in the
United Kingdom by:

Carroll & Brown Publishers Limited
20 Lonsdale Road
Queen's Park
London NW6 6RD

Text © George O'Dowd & Dragana G. Brown 2001

Recipes © Dragana G. Brown 2001

Illustrations and compilation © Carroll & Brown Limited 2001

A CIP catalogue record for this book is available from the British Library.

ISBN 1-903258-16-2

Reproduced by Colourscan, Singapore
Printed and bound in India by Ajanta
First edition

The moral rights of the George O'Dowd and Dragana G. Brown to be
identified as the authors of this work has been asserted in accordance with
the Copyright, Designs and Patents Act of 1988.

All rights reserved. No part of this publication may be reproduced in any
material form (including photocopying or storing it in any medium by
electronic means and whether or not transiently or incidentally to some
other use of this publication) without the written permission of the
copyright owner, except in accordance with the provisions of the
Copyright, Designs and Patents Act of 1988 or under the terms of a licence
issued by the Copyright Licensing Agency, 90 Tottenham Court Road,
London W1P 9HE. Applications for the copyright owner's written
permission to reproduce any part of this publication should be addressed
to the publisher.

Contents

The Road to Macrobiotics

from vice to brown rice

I first met Dragana Brown in 1986 when she was working as a waitress in a restaurant close to my manager's office where we used to sneak for meetings and afternoon teas. Healthy eating was the last thing on our minds as we chomped on Welsh Rarebit, full English breakfasts and evil French pastries. It was a time of great excess for me: I was using drugs and generally living a life of debauchery. And my diet was appalling – meat, meat and more meat.

The next time I bumped into Dragana was three years later while having a healthy lunch at the East West centre, a macrobiotic restaurant in Old Street. I was finally clean from drugs and trying desperately to sort out my diet. We started talking and exchanged numbers. Months later, Dragana and her partner Simon came to my home to interview me for a Macro magazine and we developed a lasting and rewarding friendship.

I started visiting Dragana for cooking lessons and began to realise that there was more to life than tinned soups and take away food. Before that, I could barely open a tin of baked beans and had no clue about cooking. I soon got a taste for it, though, especially when I discovered that macrobiotic food didn't just mean brown rice and lentils. In fact you can make almost any dish macrobiotic, simply by replacing certain ingredients, like meat, dairy and sugar, with more healthy ones. With Dragana's help and experience, I learnt to make food that was both healthy and exciting to eat. Once I understood the basic principles, cooking became a pleasure rather than an emotional assault course.

Tasty macrobiotic dishes are quick and easy to create

When I first stopped eating animal products back in the mid-eighties, concerned friends would ask, 'What do you live on, beans?'. The fact is, it's much easier to tell you the few foods I don't eat. Through macrobiotics, I have discovered an abundance of delicious new dishes and ingredients. One of the most exciting things about macrobiotics is the variety of foods that you can eat – and being a certified food lover, this suits me down to the ground. I have often joked that I live between meals! Above all, macrobiotics encourages you to celebrate food – so, go ahead and enjoy.

As we nibbled on our brown rice sushi rolls, we were as happy as pigs in the proverbial.

Boy George

A calmer chameleon

I started to develop digestive problems growing
up in Yugoslavia, and didn't find much solace in
conventional treatment. While training to be a
doctor and studying English at the same time,
Jimmy, one of my English professors, recommended
macrobiotics. I came to London and studied macrobiotic cooking at
the East West centre. Not only did my digestive problems clear up but, even
better, I felt more stable emotionally. Of course with four children and a
husband to look after I still have the occasional tantrum, but in general I feel
much more at peace within myself. I also have more energy.

At first I religiously followed the macrobiotic diet prescribed to me. But as
time went by, I found I could experiment more and adapt my diet to suit my
lifestyle. The basic principles of macrobiotics can be applied to any style of
cooking, and many of my recipes have been inspired by Italian, French and
traditional eastern European recipes, but adjusted to make them healthier
and more balanced.

Although I do not eat meat, have very little dairy food and only indulge in
sugar when eating out, I actually have a much more varied and satisfying
diet than I did when I ate everything. I have written this book together with
George to help others achieve the same benefits as me and make it easier to
eat natural healthy foods.

Dragana G. Brown

The macrobiotic way of life

Macrobiotics is a way of living for good health and happiness. The word itself was coined by the Japanese author and philosopher, George Ohsawa, from the Greek words *macro*, meaning 'great' or 'large' and *biotos*, meaning 'life'. The aim of macrobiotics was (and still is) to live a 'large' life – that is, to live life to the full. Exercise, positive thinking and lifestyle are all important elements of macrobiotic practice, and particular emphasis is placed on food. The macro diet is not a rigid one, but generally revolves round grains, a wide variety of vegetables, beans, sea vegetables, nuts and seeds, and soy products – all as fresh and organic as possible. These ingredients form the basis of a huge range of mouth-watering and healthful meals.

The recipes in this book have been devised for four people eating a three-course meal. Macrobiotic meals generally consist of several dishes, starting with a soup, and the idea is to eat at 90 percent capacity (if not slightly less), as over-eating is not good for your health. If you are not cooking a three-course meal, however, you may wish to increase the quantities slightly.

The ingredients in this book are very popular in Japanese cooking, but you may not be familiar with all of them. You will find tip boxes on how to prepare or cook many of the more unusual foods, and there is also a glossary of ingredients at the back of the book. Your local supermarket will stock most of these – the remainder will be available from good health food shops or Japanese stores.

Satisfying Soups

satisfying soups

from oxtail to miso

I've rarely met anyone who doesn't like a nice bowl of soup. As a child it was all tomato and oxtail but I'm pleased to tell you that I've moved on. I used to be one of those folks who bought soup in a can, but now I think of this as sacrilege. One of the first things I learnt to prepare was soup, and I have since managed to impress Dragana with my concoctions on a number of occasions. Of course, there have been hiccups, like the first time I attempted to make a split pea soup: Drags advised me to add some kombu sea vegetable, which the Japanese use in much the same way we use bay leaves. Instead of using a couple of centimetres, I tipped in a whole packet and my soup ended up looking like frog's spawn!

Soup is both refreshing and comforting, and if you have it before meals it is supposed to relax and prepare the digestive system. In macrobiotics, at least one bowl of soup a day is suggested, even at breakfast. In spring or summer, light soups such as Celery, Clear Cauliflower, or a light shoyu broth are ideal. But during the winter, soups like Barley and Garlic or Sweet Millet are heartier and more warming – in fact they can be a meal in themselves.

Soups are an essential part of the macrobiotic diet: aficionados recommend you have one or two bowls daily, delicately flavoured with miso, shoyu or seasalt.

Pesto is scrummy in soups; the hot liquid will mellow the flavour

My favourite type is Yugo Bean soup (which originates from Dragana's native Yugoslavia) – especially when Rosa, her mum, makes it (no offence Drags!). You can really experiment with soups and allow your adventurous side to shine. I'm a huge fan of ginger and love to use exotic ingredients such as lemon grass and cumin, which as a child I thought were foreign countries.

Soups like miso are regarded as medicinal and are excellent for digestive complaints and stamina. On tour I crave miso soup and will take the instant packets just in case, but there's nothing like the real McCoy.

Basic Miso Soup

4-cm piece dried wakame

1 medium onion, sliced into half moons

100g carrots, diced or sliced diagonally

4 tsp miso paste

small handful of watercress, finely chopped

¼ sheet nori, finely cut, for decoration

Pre-soak the wakame in cold water for 2 minutes. Remove and chop into small pieces. Place in a 1-litre saucepan with 750ml water and bring to the boil. Add the sliced onion. Lower the heat and simmer for 2 minutes. Add the carrot and simmer for another 2 minutes. Turn off the heat.

Put the miso paste and 2 tbsp cold water into a cup. Stir well to make sure all the bits are broken and the mixture is smooth.

Gently reheat the vegetable mixture and add the diluted miso paste. Simmer for about 3 minutes. Just before the end of the cooking time, add the chopped watercress. To make the nori decoration, I use scissors to cut it into fine strips about 30 x 2 mm. But you can make small squares, thick strips or whatever looks good to you. Ladle the soup into bowls and sprinkle with a few finely cut pieces of nori.

High temperatures destroy some of the beneficial enzymes in miso, so make sure that the soup is not bubbling when you add the miso paste.

This particular recipe is how miso soup is made traditionally, but any soup – from leek and potato to minestrone – can be miso soup, all you have to do is add miso. Any kind of miso paste can be used for this recipe; but our favourite is barley miso.

miso paste

Creamy Celery Soup

Heat the oil in a 2-litre saucepan, add the chopped onion and sauté for 1 minute, stirring with a pair of chopsticks. Dip the chopsticks in the salt and stir the onion again. Add the celery and 2 tbsp water. Cover the pan and continue cooking for 1 minute.

Add 500ml water to the pan, bring to the boil, then reduce the heat to medium and simmer for 15 minutes. Turn off the heat, liquidise the soup in a food processor, then return it to the saucepan, add soy cream and simmer for 1–2 minutes. Leave to stand for 5 minutes before serving.

1 tbsp sunflower oil
1 large or 2 small onions, chopped
sea salt
350g celery, roughly chopped
2 tbsp soy cream

If the celery you are using is stringy, sieve the soup after processing.

Potato Soup

Place 1½ litres water and the diced potatoes in a large saucepan. Cover and bring to the boil. Lower the heat and simmer for 10–15 minutes (the longer you cook the potatoes, the richer the soup will be). Add the carrots and cook for a further 5–10 minutes. Next, add the oil, sea salt and pepper to the pan. Simmer the mixture for a minute, then switch off the heat and add the Chinese cabbage. Leave to stand for 3–5 minutes, and serve garnished with the flat-leaf parsley.

300g potatoes, finely diced
150g carrots, diced
1 tbsp olive oil
1 tsp sea salt (or to taste)
¼ tsp white pepper
150g Chinese cabbage
fresh flat-leaf parsley, for decoration

Barley and Garlic Soup

200g barley, washed
100g carrots, diced
75g celery, diced
½ clove garlic, crushed
1 tbsp sesame oil
sea salt
garlic sourdough croutons (see page 32)
fresh parsley, for decoration

Prepare the barley a day in advance. Place the barley and 600ml water in a 1-litre saucepan. Simmer for 10–15 minutes. Spoon into a bowl along with any remaining water, cool and refrigerate until ready to use.

When ready to cook, place the barley, carrot and celery in a 2-litre saucepan, and cover with twice as much water as their depth. Bring to the boil then lower the heat and simmer for 15–20 minutes. Add the garlic, oil and sea salt to taste. Simmer for another 5 minutes.

Serve the soup with a few garlic croutons and decorate with the parsley.

To make this soup richer in the cold winter months, I like to use toasted sesame oil. This also gives the soup a wonderful nutty aroma.

French Onion Soup

In a 2-litre saucepan, heat the sesame oil over a high heat, then add the sliced onion. Stir with a pair of chopsticks, then dip them in the sea salt and stir the onion again; cook for 2–3 minutes.

Add the Cognac. Lower the heat to medium and simmer for a couple of minutes, stirring occasionally. Add 1 litre water, cover and bring to the boil. Lower the heat and simmer for 10 minutes. Reduce the heat to low.

Meanwhile, make the croutons. Heat up the oil in a deep-fat fryer, add the cubes of bread and fry until golden.

Dilute the miso with 1 tbsp cold water in a cup. Add the miso to the soup. Cook over a very low heat for 2 minutes. Ladle the soup into serving bowls and sprinkle with sourdough croutons to serve.

1 tbsp sesame oil
2 large onions, sliced in half moons
sea salt
5 tbsp good-quality Cognac
sunflower oil for deep-frying
4 slices sourdough bread cut into 2-cm cubes
4 tsp barley miso

Sourdough bread is normally prepared with a special sourdough starter instead of yeast. You can make a sourdough starter yourself using a mixture of flour and water: simply leave it to ferment uncovered for a few days. Then you just take a handful of this mixture and mix it with the bread dough.

Yugo Bean Soup

200g dried haricot beans (or organic sugar-free tinned beans)
3 bay leaves
1 small onion, sliced
50g carrots, diced
50g celery, diced
50g parsnips, diced
1 tsp sea salt
2 tbsp sunflower oil
1tbsp organic unbleached white flour
1 tsp shichimi
(also known as 7 spice)
flat-leaf parsley, for decoration

If you are using dried beans, prepare them a day in advance by rinsing and then placing them in a large covered saucepan with 1200ml warm water. Soak the beans overnight.

When ready to use, heat the beans and water and bring to the boil. Boil for a couple of minutes, then drain and discard the water. Rinse the beans and place in a 2.5-litre saucepan. Add 1 litre water, the bay leaves and onion and bring to the boil. Cook, covered, over a high heat for about 10 minutes.

Add the carrot, celery and parsnip to the beans. Lower the heat to medium and simmer for another 30 minutes with the lid slightly to one side so that the steam can escape easily. After about 20 minutes, add a further 200ml water and the sea salt.

Meanwhile, put the oil and flour in a small saucepan or frying pan, heat gently, and stir constantly for about 2 minutes so the flour does not burn. Add the mixture to the beans, stir well and simmer for another 2 minutes.

Before serving, put a pinch of shichimi in each soup bowl, and then add the soup. Decorate with the flat-leaf parsley.

This is one of the most popular traditional soups in Yugoslavia – hence its name. When cooking beans, don't add salt to the cooking water, as it makes the beans tough and they will take longer to cook.

Shoyu Soup
with Carrot and Radish

18-cm piece dried kombu
4 dried shiitake mushrooms
50g carrots, cut into fine strips
**50g celery, cut in thin
strips diagonally**
1 bunch radishes, thinly sliced
150ml shoyu (or to taste)
nori, cut into strips, for decoration

Pour 1 litre cold water into a 2-litre saucepan and bring to the boil. Add the kombu and shiitake mushrooms to the pan, lower the heat and simmer for about 10 minutes.

Remove the kombu (and reuse in other dishes: see page 20) and the mushrooms from the pan. Slice the mushrooms thinly, discarding the stalks. Put them back in the pan together with the carrot, celery and radishes. Season with shoyu to taste and simmer for another minute.

Turn off the heat and leave the soup to stand for 3–4 minutes. This allows the vegetables to cook for a bit longer, but they will still have a little bite. Garnish with the nori just before serving.

Shoyu is a strong salty liquid seasoning. It is best to start with less, taste first and then add more if needed.

Minestrone Soup

Place the leeks, carrot, celery, cabbage, French beans and haricot beans in a 2-litre saucepan. Slowly add 1 litre water. Cover and bring to the boil. Reduce the heat to medium and simmer for 10–15 minutes. Add the sea salt, cauliflower, broccoli and pasta. Cook for another 5 minutes or until the pasta is soft.

In a small bowl, mix the garlic, olive oil and basil together. Add a pinch of sea salt. Divide the mixture between 4 soup bowls and pour the hot soup over it. Leave to stand for 3–4 minutes, so the garlic cooks a little bit. Mix the soup thoroughly before eating.

60g leeks, diced

50g carrots, cut into half moon slices

25g celery, sliced diagonally into 1-cm pieces

70g cabbage, cut into 1-cm squares

6 French beans, cut into thirds

100g organic tinned haricot beans (or chickpeas or kidney beans)

1 tsp sea salt

30g cauliflower florets, cut into smaller florets

30g broccoli florets, cut into smaller florets

60g mini wholemeal pasta shells

1 small clove garlic, crushed

1 tbsp olive oil

handful fresh basil, finely chopped

Since you are not actually cooking the garlic in the soup, its taste can be very strong. By leaving it in the hot soup for a few minutes before eating, its flavour will mellow.

Cucumber and Ginger Soup

5 dried shiitake mushrooms
1 piece kombu, 3 x 3-cm
1 tbsp sesame oil
30g spring onions, cut diagonally into 1-cm pieces
2-cm piece ginger, cut into matchsticks
sea salt
130g cucumber, washed, halved and cut into thin half moon slices
150g tofu, cut into 1.5-cm squares
2 tbsp cornflour
fresh coriander, for decoration

Pre-soak the shiitake mushrooms and kombu in 150ml cold water for 5–10 minutes. Reserve the soaking water. Discard the stems from the mushrooms. Cut the mushrooms and the kombu into squares.

Heat the oil in a 1-litre saucepan. Add the spring onions and ginger and stir with a pair of chopsticks. Dip the chopsticks in sea salt and use to stir the onions and ginger over a high heat for about a minute. Add the mushrooms and cucumber and sauté for another minute. Now add the kombu and reserved soaking water and tofu, and simmer for about 2–3 minutes. Pour in 750ml water, cover and bring to the boil.

Meanwhile, mix the cornflour with 50ml cold water to make a paste.

As soon as the soup boils, remove the lid, add the cornflour mixture and 1 tsp sea salt and simmer over a very low heat for a few minutes. Garnish with fresh coriander.

If you prefer this soup thicker, add 1–2 tbsp extra cornflour paste. You could also increase the amount of ginger on a cold day.

Kombu, *also known as giant sea kelp, has long, dried fronds and adds flavour to this soup. You can reuse it two or three times before it loses its flavour: leave it to dry in between. It is particularly good with pulses, as it helps them to cook more quickly. Just place it in a pan with the beans or peas and water and cook the pulses as normal.*

bg

Normally you think of cucumber as being cold and chopped up in a salad. But it works really well in this hot, warming dish. The cucumber is calming and the ginger is stimulating: it's a bit like waltzing in slingbacks. A delicious contradiction!

Lentil and Cumin Soup

**200g green lentils (other kinds
are equally good)**

**100g carrots, sliced diagonally
into 1-cm pieces**

**70g celery, sliced diagonally
into 1-cm pieces**

2 bay leaves

1 tsp sea salt

2 tbsp sunflower oil

½ tsp cumin

½ tsp turmeric

5 fresh shiitake mushrooms, sliced

**30g spring onions, finely
sliced diagonally**

4 slices lemon

Prepare the lentils a day in advance. Wash lentils then place in a saucepan with 1 litre warm water and cover. Leave to soak overnight.

When ready to use, bring the lentils to the boil, covered, using the same water, and cook for about 10 minutes. Turn the heat off, and drain the lentils.

Put the carrots and celery into a 2-litre saucepan and place the lentils on top. Add the bay leaves and carefully pour over 1 litre water. Cover, and bring to the boil. Reduce the heat to medium and simmer for 15–20 minutes. Halfway through the cooking time, add the sea salt.

Meanwhile, heat the oil, cumin and turmeric in a small saucepan and fry for 1–2 minutes. Add the shiitake mushrooms and spring onions and sauté for another minute. Pour the mixture into the soup and simmer for 1–2 minutes.

Serve the soup with a slice of lemon in each bowl. Just before eating, press the lemon with your spoon a little to release the juice.

Although green lentils cook easily, I prefer to soak them first, as they are easier on the digestive system when pre-soaked.

Parsnip and Pear Soup

1 tbsp sunflower oil
1 small onion, sliced
sea salt
350g parsnips, chopped
100g pears, chopped
coriander leaves, for decoration

Heat the oil in a 2-litre saucepan and add the onion. Add a pinch of sea salt. Sauté over a high heat for a minute or so. Add 1 tbsp water and continue to sauté for another minute. Add the parsnip and 1 litre water. Cover and bring to the boil. Reduce the heat to medium, and simmer for about 10 minutes.

Add the pear and cook for another 5 minutes until the parsnip is soft. Remove from the heat and put in a blender or food processor. Process until well blended, then return the mixture to the pan. Add more water, if the soup seems too thick, and reheat. Season to taste with sea salt and simmer for 1–2 minutes. Serve garnished with the coriander leaves.

Choose ripe or even over-ripe pears for this recipe: they are sweeter and cook more easily.

We all need sweetness in our lives, but rather than digging into chocolate bars and other sugary foods, try this soup instead. The parsnips and pears are sweet enough to satisfy your cravings, and are also very calming.

Drita's Soup

Cut all the vegetables into large chunks. In a large saucepan, heat the oil over a high heat and sauté the onion for a minute, then add all the other vegetables except for the cauliflower and savoy cabbage. Sauté for another minute.

Pour over enough water to cover the vegetables. Cover the pan and bring to the boil. Add the cauliflower and savoy cabbage leaves. Sprinkle in a pinch of salt and cook, with the lid slightly to one side so steam can escape, over a medium to high heat for 10–15 minutes or until the vegetables are soft. Turn the heat off and leave to cool for a few minutes.

Pour the mixture into a blender or food processor and liquidise until smooth. Return the soup to the pan. Add more water, if the soup seems too thick, and sea salt to taste. Simmer over a low heat for a couple of minutes. Add the millet, if using, and serve garnished with the parsley.

2 tbsp sunflower oil
1 medium onion
50g parsnips
50g carrots
20g celery
50g white cabbage
5-cm piece daikon
100g cauliflower
3 medium savoy cabbage leaves
sea salt
fresh parsley, for decoration
4 tbsp cooked millet (optional)

Daikon (also known as mooli) is a long, white radish. Its pungent taste is the perfect foil for the sweetness of the other vegetables in this dish.

Drita is a Yugoslavian friend who taught me how to make this soup. The dish is even tastier if you add cooked millet just before serving.

Creamy Carrot Soup

1 tbsp sesame oil
1 medium onion, diced
500g carrots, cut into large chunks
50g cauliflower florets
sea salt
150g cooked left-over oats or rice
2 tbsp soy cream
¼ tsp cumin

This is great for those cold winter weeks. More filling than an ordinary carrot soup, thanks to the addition of the oats or rice, it is also very soothing.

Heat the oil in a 2-litre saucepan over a high heat and add the onion. Sauté for 2 minutes. Then add the carrots, cauliflower florets and a pinch of sea salt. Slowly pour over 1 litre water then cover and bring to the boil. Reduce the heat to medium-low and simmer for about 15 minutes (or until the vegetables are soft). Turn off the heat and allow the mixture to cool slightly.

Put the vegetable mixture into a blender or food processor and process until smooth. Return to the saucepan, adding more water if required. Add the oats or rice, soy cream and cumin. Simmer for a minute longer and serve.

Sweet Millet Soup

100g millet, washed

100g sweet pumpkin (kabucha is best), cut into chunks

50g carrots, diced

50g parsnips, diced

1 small onion

sea salt

1 small spring onion, very finely sliced diagonally, for decoration

Heat a heavy-based frying pan over a high heat and add the millet. Dry-fry for 3–5 minutes or until the millet is golden in colour, stirring frequently to prevent it from burning.

In a large saucepan, place the pumpkin, carrot, parsnip and onion, then top with the millet. Pour in enough water to stand 2cm above the vegetables. Cover the pan and gently bring to the boil, then reduce the heat to medium-low and simmer for about 20–30 minutes. The millet expands during cooking, so you'll need to keep adding water to make sure it is covered.

Season with sea salt, turn the heat to low and add another 300–600ml water. When the millet is cooked (it should be soft), turn off the heat. Serve the soup garnished with the sliced spring onion.

Pumpkin You really need to use a sweet pumpkin for this recipe. Green Japanese kabucha is the best type to use if you can get hold of it. If you can find only the more common orange pumpkin, ask your greengrocer how sweet it is likely to be. You don't need to peel the kabucha for this dish as the peel is quite sweet. Simply scrub well with a vegetable brush.

Millet is one of the sweetest grains, and is much softer than rice or wheat. This soup is very good if you are suffering from any kind of digestive problem, and also has a fantastically grounding effect. To make a richer soup, fry the millet in a bit of sesame oil – or, richer still, toasted sesame oil.

Clear Cauliflower Soup

Place the wakame in a dish and soak in 300ml water for 5 minutes. Remove the wakame, reserving the water, and chop into small pieces. Pour the reserved soaking water into a 1-litre measuring jug and top up to the 1 litre mark with cold water. Pour the liquid into a large saucepan and add the wakame. Cover the pan and bring to the boil. Reduce the heat to medium and simmer for 5 minutes. Add the cauliflower and simmer for another 5 minutes. Season with shoyu and add the nori. Simmer for 2 more minutes, then turn off the heat.

Serve garnished with parsley and 2 carrot flowers (see below) in each bowl.

1 piece dried wakame, 15 x 2-cm
350g cauliflower, cut into florets
75ml shoyu (or to taste)
1 sheet nori, cut into 3-cm fine strips
parsley, for decoration
1 medium-sized carrot, for decoration

This soup looks really attractive with a few carrot flowers floating on the top. To make them, use a knife to cut 4 or 5 long grooves from a medium-sized carrot, and then thinly slice it crosswise.

Magnificent Mains

Magnificent Mains

oodles of noodles

Becoming macrobiotic doesn't mean you have to forgo your favourite foods: all you need to do is to make a few adaptations. For example, you can take something really traditional like a pasta with tomato sauce and basil and make it macro friendly. In fact, learning to make quick and tasty pasta sauces is a Godsend when you have a busy schedule. You can also be ingenious and cook the pasta the night before to save time.

Variety in your diet is key: if you eat the same things all the time, you will end up at the nearest fast food outlet!

Some of my favourite main course dishes are Sizzling soba, which I could easily live on, and Drags' Garlic Rice, which is all about elbow power (according to Dragana), but I suspect she says that because she doesn't always feel like making it. The Tofu Steaks and Deep-fried Rice Balls are ideal for recovering meat-eaters. Some of the main course recipes might seem like you need

a science degree, but once you know what not to use and stock your cupboards with the necessary ingredients, it does become easier. I used to walk around health food stores with a disturbed expression thinking, 'What's seitan' or 'Where do I find a shiitake mushroom?' I would never have contemplated using polenta or many of the grains suggested in this book. But now I realise how boring my life was!

Certain dishes work better during hot spells (which are very seldom in the UK). You wouldn't want a stew or a casserole on a bright summer's day; ideally you'd be tucking into cous cous or light pasta dishes instead. In the winter you will probably gravitate towards hearty dishes that warm your internal oven.

Deep-frying the Tempura Noodle Sushi – recipe on page 52

Banishing Barley Stew

200g barley, washed and
pre-soaked in cold water
for 2–3 hours or overnight

1 small onion, diced

100g carrots, diced

50g celery, diced

40g dried tofu, pre-soaked
and diced

sea salt

sesame oil

4 slices sourdough rice or
barley bread

1 clove garlic, halved

fresh flat-leaf parsley, for
decoration

Place the barley into a large saucepan. Cover with water to twice the barley's depth. Cook for 20–30 minutes, checking every now and again to make sure that there is enough water.

Into a heavy cast-iron saucepan, layer the vegetables, tofu and barley in the following order: onion, carrot, celery, tofu and pre-cooked barley. Cover with twice as much water (use the tofu soaking water, too) and cook on a medium–low heat for 40–60 minutes, adding water from time to time.

Season with sea salt. (Always add a small amount, taste, and then add more, if necessary.) Simmer for an additional 10 minutes, turn off the heat and cover the pan. The stew should be creamy and moist, not watery.

In a frying pan (preferably cast-iron), pour just enough sesame oil to cover the surface of the pan. Fry each slice of bread for a couple of minutes on each side on a medium to high heat. Remove the bread and rub the cut garlic clove on both sides.

Put the bread slices in a large bowl and pour the rest of the stew ingredients on top. If you like, decorate with a few parsley leaves.

The garlic will impart more flavour to the bread if you rub it over as soon as the bread is removed from the pan.

This dish is great for ridding the body of excess animal and dairy fats, which is why I like to call it Banishing Barley Stew. Its creamy quality is very relaxing, especially for the spleen, and it's a good cold weather dish. As a child, I was served up stew on a regular basis – and to be honest, I grew to loathe stew – but looking back I realise that it made me strong.

Emerald Eye Stew

Place 1 litre water, the mushrooms, miso, shoyu and ginger slices in a flameproof casserole. Slowly bring to the boil, then reduce the heat and remove the mushrooms. Cut the stems off, discard, then slice the caps. Put them back in the casserole. Add the beans and broccoli and simmer for 2 minutes.

Meanwhile, heat the oil in a frying pan and fry the tofu for a couple of minutes. Remove the tofu using a slotted spoon and place in the casserole.

Briefly fry the garlic in the frying pan and add it to the stew along with any remaining oil. Add the pak choy, watercress and Chinese cabbage to the casserole and turn the heat to low.

In a cup, mix the arrowroot with 2 tbsp cold water and stir until smooth. Add it to the stew, stirring constantly to prevent lumps. It should only take a few minutes for the stew to thicken. Serve on top of cooked cous cous.

3 dried shiitake mushrooms
2 tbsp white miso
2 tbsp shoyu
2-cm piece ginger, unpeeled and cut into 4–5 thin slices
50g runner or French beans
50g broccoli
1tbsp sesame oil
200g tofu, cut into 3-cm squares
1 small clove garlic, crushed
50g pak choy, cut into 2-cm squares
50g watercress, cut into 2-cm squares
1 Chinese cabbage leaf, cut into 2-cm squares
1 tbsp arrowroot
cooked cous cous to serve

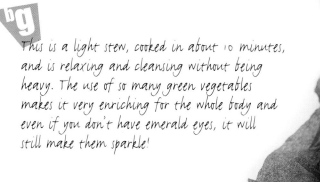

dried shiitake mushrooms

This is a light stew, cooked in about 10 minutes, and is relaxing and cleansing without being heavy. The use of so many green vegetables makes it very enriching for the whole body and even if you don't have emerald eyes, it will still make them sparkle!

Nabe

500g udon (or soba) noodles

1 piece kombu, 4 x 2-cm

3–4 dried shiitake mushrooms, pre-soaked and sliced, stem discarded

1 medium carrot, cut diagonally into thin slices

1 small leek, cut diagonally into 2-cm pieces

4 spring onions, halved

2 Chinese cabbage leaves (or other leafy greens), cut into large squares

4 small broccoli florets

4 small cauliflower florets

4-cm piece daikon, cut into matchsticks

250g tofu

FOR THE SAUCE

1 tsp black sesame seeds

90ml shoyu

1 tbsp brown rice vinegar

1-cm piece ginger, grated

Cook the noodles according to the packet instructions, but leave them slightly underdone (a minute or so less than the recommended cooking time). Drain and reserve.

Meanwhile, prepare the sauce. Wash the sesame seeds under a little running water. Heat up a frying pan, add the sesame seeds and toast them, stirring constantly, until they start to pop (about 3–5 minutes). Remove from the heat immediately, and mix the seeds with the other sauce ingredients in a bowl.

Fill up a nabe pot or a large, heavy-based flameproof casserole with water to within 4–5cm from the top. Add the kombu and mushrooms. Bring to the boil, covered, on a medium to high heat. Reduce the heat to very low, remove the kombu and gradually add the rest of the vegetables, tofu and noodles. Cover the pot and continue cooking. When steam starts to come out of the hole in the lid (or after about 3–4 minutes), the nabe is ready.

To serve, divide the sauce between 4 serving bowls and add a ladleful of broth from the nabe pot to each.

Transfer the nabe pot to the table. Use chopsticks to help yourselves to cooked ingredients from the nabe pot a mouthful at a time, dipping them into the sauce in your bowls as you do so.

*This recipe is named after the traditional
earthenware Japanese pot or 'nabe' in which it is
usually cooked. It is best if this dish is cooked at
the table on a small gas burner. However, it can
be cooked just as easily on the hob.*

Jelena's Gung-ho Goulash

2 tbsp sunflower or sesame oil
3 medium onions, finely diced
3 tbsp unbleached white flour
150g carrots, diced
250g seitan, finely chopped
1 tsp sea salt
¼ tsp black pepper
3 tbsp chopped fresh parsley
shichimi (to taste)
mashed potato or pasta, to serve

In a large saucepan, heat the oil and sauté the onions for a couple of minutes. Add the flour and stir for another minute. Add 1 litre water and bring to the boil. Lower the heat and simmer for about 10 minutes.

Add the carrots and seitan and cook for another 5–10 minutes. Season with sea salt and black pepper and add the parsley. Simmer for another minute and season with shichimi, if you like a spicy flavour. Serve with some mashed potato or pasta.

sesame oil

Seitan wheat This is wheat protein that has been separated from the starch and bran by kneading and washing and then cooked in a mixture of shoyu, water, kombu and ginger. It is easy to make, but you can also buy it ready-made in good healthfood shops.

Jelena is my sister – who is a very good cook. This is her variation on a traditional Yugoslavian recipe.

Tofu Garlic Steaks

Preheat the oven to 230°C/gas 8. Mix the olive oil, garlic, lemon grass, coriander, breadcrumbs, seven spice (if you are using it) and sea salt in a bowl.

In a separate bowl mix the tahini, umeboshi paste and mustard with a few drops of water to make the mixture slightly creamy.

Place the tofu slices on a baking sheet and spread a teaspoon of the tahini mixture on each piece of tofu. Then spread the breadcrumb mixture on top and transfer to the oven. Bake for 15 minutes.

Serve with steamed green vegetables such as broccoli, kale and watercress, and with natural pickles (sour gherkins are our favourite).

3–4 tsp olive oil

2 garlic cloves crushed

2 lemon grass sticks, finely chopped

4 tsp coriander, finely chopped

6 tsp wholemeal natural breadcrumbs

1 tsp Japanese seven spice or shichimi (optional)

¼ tsp sea salt

1 tsp light tahini (crushed sesame seeds)

½ tsp umeboshi paste

2 tsp natural mustard (with no sugar or honey)

2 packets of organic tofu, drained and each cut in half horizontally

Umeboshi paste is made from pickled umeboshi plums. It is very strong on its own – it has a distinctive salty, sour taste – but used sparingly, as in this recipe, it really brings out the flavours of the other ingredients. Don't add salt to the finished dish until you have tasted it: you will probably discover that it is salty enough already.

Marinated Mini Tofu Steaks

700g tofu, cut into 7-mm slices

sesame or sunflower oil

25g white flour

FOR THE MARINADE

1 clove garlic, crushed

1 tsp shichimi

2 small spring onions, trimmed and sliced on the diagonal

4 tbsp mirin (Japanese sweet rice seasoning) or sake

150ml shoyu

1 tsp black sesame seeds

FOR THE DIPPING SAUCE

45ml shoyu

2-cm piece ginger, peeled and grated finely

2.5-cm piece daikon, grated

Place all the marinade ingredients into a large shallow dish and mix well. Arrange the tofu slices in the dish, cover and leave at room temperature for 30 minutes. Turn the slices over and marinade for a further 30 minutes.

In another bowl, mix all the dipping sauce ingredients together. Cover and set aside.

Add just enough oil to coat the bottom of a medium-sized frying pan and heat. Remove the tofu steaks from the marinade and dip in the flour. Cook the steaks, in batches, for 3 minutes on each side (you may need to add more oil when cooking subsequent batches). Drain on kitchen roll and serve with the sauce and any remaining marinade.

Tofu is a soybean curd rich in protein, vitamins, minerals and calcium. You can buy it fresh or dried, but for this dish use the fresh variety, which comes prepacked in a little water. Drain it well and pat it dry before cooking. If you don't use the whole packet, keep the rest in the fridge covered in plenty of water (change daily).

Light but filling, this is a good dish if you are planning a night down the disco or a game of squash (not that I play much squash, but I do go to an awful lot of discos!).

D *Without thoughtful preparation, tofu can be very bland – but these steaks are anything but bland. The tofu soaks up the marinade and the flour coating adds richness which leaves the tofu soft in the middle and crispy on the outside.*

Krista's 'Perfect Pose' Pasta

500g penne pasta
1 tsp sea salt
5 tbsp olive oil
3 cloves garlic, crushed
1 small red chilli, finely diced
450g tomatoes, roughly chopped and seasoned with ½ tsp sea salt
60g whole black olives
2 tbsp capers
1 tbsp chopped fresh flat-leaf parsley, for decoration

Cook the pasta according to the packet instructions. Add ½ tsp sea salt and 1 tsp olive oil to the cooking water. When *al dente* (still has a little 'bite'), drain the pasta and rinse thoroughly with cold water. Set aside.

Combine the remaining oil, crushed garlic, chopped chilli and a pinch of sea salt in a deep frying pan or saucepan. Cook on a low heat for 2 minutes, stirring constantly. Add the chopped tomatoes, olives and capers and cook for a further 10 minutes. Add the cooked pasta and ½ tsp sea salt, toss to coat the pasta in the sauce, cover and leave to stand for 1–2 minutes. Add the parsley and serve immediately.

Krista is a friend from the United States, who has appeared on a cooking show hosted by Oprah Winfrey. Krista won first prize! When I stayed with her, she shared this recipe with me.

Fuss-free Fusilli

500g organic fusilli pasta
3 tbsp olive oil
1 clove garlic, chopped
sea salt
150g tomatoes, roughly chopped
2 tbsp chopped fresh basil, for decoration

Prepare all the ingredients first. Cook the pasta according to the packet instructions. Drain and while still hot, tip into a bowl and add the olive oil and garlic and mix well. Season with sea salt according to taste and swiftly add the tomatoes and the basil. Serve immediately.

Creamy Shiitake Pasta

Cook the pasta according to the packet instructions. When *al dente*, drain and reserve.

Meanwhile, in a wok or a large frying pan, heat the oil until very hot but not burning before adding the mushrooms and the spring onions and stir-fry for a minute or two. Add 1 tbsp soy cream, the pasta, sea salt and black pepper and toss. Pour in the rest of the soy cream and mix well, then decorate with the fresh parsley. Serve while hot.

500g organic fusilli pasta
1 tbsp olive oil
80g fresh shiitake mushrooms, sliced
100g spring onions, cut into 1.5-cm diagonal pieces
150ml soy cream
1 tsp sea salt
½ tsp black pepper, freshly ground
2 tbsp fresh flat-leaf parsley, finely chopped, for decoration

This is perfect when you fancy something rich and creamy but don't want the guilt of eating real cream, and it proves that you don't have to smother pasta in dairy products to satisfy those creamy cravings. If you don't tell your guests you're using soy cream, they will never know!

fresh shiitake mushrooms

Soy cream is a non-dairy product made from whole soy beans. It is low in saturated fats and cholesterol and makes a much healthier alternative to dairy cream.

Lorenzo's Pasta

500g organic spaghetti
2 tbsp olive oil
3 large cloves garlic, each cut into 2–3 large pieces
450g jar organic sugar-free tomato sauce
1 tsp sea salt
1 tsp maple syrup
black pepper, to taste
30g fresh basil, chopped

Cook the pasta according to the packet instructions. Drain and rinse very lightly with boiling water.

While the pasta is cooking, heat the oil in a large saucepan and fry the garlic for a few minutes over a medium to high heat. If you don't like garlic, remove it from the pan now – the oil will have taken on only a subtle garlic flavour.

Add the tomato sauce, salt, maple syrup and black pepper to the pan. Cook for 3–4 minutes then add the chopped basil. Add the pasta to the sauce, and toss well before serving to coat the pasta in the sauce.

This particular pasta dish comes courtesy of my Italian friend Lorenzo. Observing the way other people cook can be very useful. Sometimes the simplest thing, like Lorenzo's method of frying large chunks of garlic on a high heat, can make all the difference to the success of a dish. When it comes to pasta, the Italians certainly know a thing or two. Normally he would use sugar instead of maple syrup, but maple syrup is just as sweet as sugar and much healthier. Rice and corn syrup would be even better!

Sizzling Soba

500g soba noodles
1 tbsp sesame oil
1 small onion, sliced
50g carrots, cut into matchsticks
50g celery
4 Chinese cabbage leaves, sliced
4 tbsp shoyu
3-cm piece ginger, grated

Cook the noodles according to the packet instructions. Drain and rinse thoroughly.

Heat the oil in a large wok or frying pan until hot. Add the onion and stir-fry for 1 minute, then add the carrots and the celery. Stir-fry for a few minutes. Add the noodles, mixing them well with the vegetables, followed by the Chinese cabbage and season with shoyu. Remove from the heat. Squeeze the juice of the grated ginger over the mixture and serve immediately.

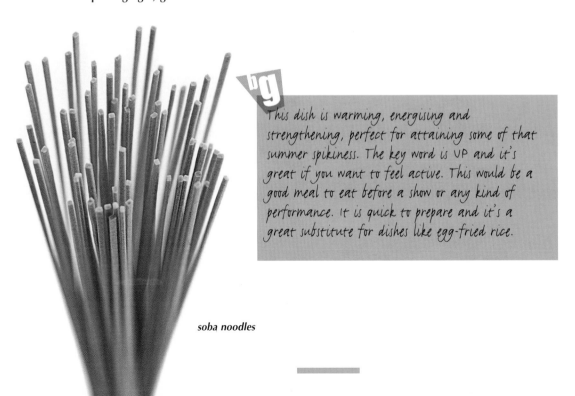

soba noodles

This dish is warming, energising and strengthening, perfect for attaining some of that summer spikiness. The key word is UP and it's great if you want to feel active. This would be a good meal to eat before a show or any kind of performance. It is quick to prepare and it's a great substitute for dishes like egg-fried rice.

Cous Cous with Tofu and Vegetables

First make a marinade by mixing the shoyu and vinegar together. Place the cut-up tofu in a bowl, cover with the marinade and leave it for about 10 minutes, turning it over occasionally.

Add 600ml water to a large saucepan and bring to the boil. Add a pinch of sea salt. Turn off the heat and add the cous cous. Cover and leave to soak for 20 minutes.

Meanwhile, heat the oil in a large, heavy saucepan or wok. Add the marinated tofu and onion, and stir with a pair of chopsticks. Dip the tips of the chopsticks into the sea salt, then continue to stir the onion and tofu with them. Fry for a few minutes, stirring the whole time. Add the carrots and celery and stir well. Cook for a further few minutes, then add the peas and sweetcorn. Cook for another 3–4 minutes, then turn off the heat. Stir in the cous cous. Season with the shoyu and garnish with a few chive stems.

2 tbsp shoyu
1 tbsp brown rice vinegar
250g tofu, cut into 1-cm squares
sea salt
225g cous cous
2 tbsp sesame oil
100g onion, diced
50g carrots, diced
25g celery, diced
80g peas (fresh or frozen)
80g sweetcorn kernels (fresh or frozen)
3 tbsp shoyu
chive stems, for decoration

If you like strong flavours, you can leave the tofu in the marinade for longer, say half an hour, or alternatively add another tablespoon of shoyu to the marinade.

This dish is also great with seitan (which makes it richer) but tofu is generally more available. It is a very filling recipe, and using a good-quality grain such as cous cous rather than potatoes or bread will make it lighter and easier on the digestion. Being a fan of potatoes (sorry, I'm Irish) and a lover of bread, I find dishes like this can satisfy those occasional cravings for stodgy meals.

Noodles in Shoyu Broth

750g udon (or soba) noodles
1 piece kombu, 3 x 2-cm
4 small dried shiitake mushrooms
¼ tsp sea salt
1 small onion, sliced in half moons
50g carrots, cut into matchsticks
75ml shoyu
1 tbsp mirin or sake
1tbsp sesame oil
4 blocks mochi (see page 48)
**1 small spring onion, finely
cut diagonally**
2 sheets nori, cut into strips
shichimi to taste

Cook the noodles according to the packet instructions. When the noodles are cooked, rinse them in cold water and set aside. Rinse the saucepan out and then refill it with 1 litre water, bring it to the boil, then turn off the heat and keep it covered (you will use this later to reheat the noodles).

To make the broth, place 1 litre water, the kombu, mushrooms and sea salt into a 2-litre saucepan. Bring to the boil over a medium to high heat. Simmer for 5 minutes then remove the kombu. Save the kombu for another dish (it is very good with beans). Take out the mushrooms, discard the stems, slice the caps and put the mushrooms back in the pan. Add the onion, cook for 5 minutes then add the carrot. Cook for another 2 minutes. Season with shoyu and mirin (or sake). Simmer for another minute over a low heat then turn off the heat.

Heat the sesame oil in a cast-iron frying pan. When the oil is hot, add the mochi. Cover and fry for about 2 minutes over a medium heat. Turn the mochi over and cook for another 2 minutes. Remove to a plate.

When just ready to serve, dip the noodles into the hot water to reheat, then drain. Divide the noodles between 4 deep bowls. Top each with a block of mochi and pour over the broth. Garnish each bowl with spring onions and nori strips. Let everyone help themselves to shichimi.

Guilt-free Polenta Mash

900ml soy milk
1 tbsp olive oil
1 tsp sea salt
225g polenta
10 black Kalamata olives
50g oil-preserved sun-dried
tomatoes, drained and chopped
1 block mochi, grated
basil leaves, for decoration

Combine the milk, olive oil and the sea salt in a 2-litre heavy saucepan. Bring to the boil. Reduce the heat to low and slowly pour in the polenta, whisking it constantly. After about 3 minutes, add the olives, sun-dried tomatoes and mochi. Stir for another minute, then turn off the heat. The mash should be creamy – if it is not, mix in a little more soy milk. Transfer the mixture to a serving dish and garnish with some basil leaves.

Back on the subject of potatoes, this way of preparing polenta is a great substitute for traditional creamy mashed potatoes. You can devour it without worrying about the slab of butter that would usually be included. The sun-dried tomatoes and olives add a bit of extra salt and the grated mochi melts down like cheese.

Mochi is pounded sweet brown rice and comes in blocks, which can be grated and melted over dishes instead of cheese or it can be fried and served with a dressing. Always remember that mochi must be cooked, and don't be put off by the fact that in its dry form it looks like plastic!

Fried Polenta 'Chips'

It's best to prepare the polenta in the morning or even the day before an evening meal. For thicker chips, you can cool it in a deep bowl, but the cooling will take longer.

You can fry the polenta without the maize meal, but with it, you get a crispier texture. If, like me, you enjoy fried food, this dish can satisfy a craving for traditional chips. By adding good-quality (sugar-free) baked beans, you get to eat like a real lumberjack and by preparing the polenta beforehand, you can rustle up this dish in no time. Yee-ha!

Place 1 litre cold water and a pinch of salt in a 3-litre saucepan. Bring to a boil, then remove from the heat. Slowly, whisk the polenta into the water and put the pan back on a low heat, over a flame diffuser. Cover and cook for 10–15 minutes, whisking every 5 minutes or so, until thick.

Spoon the polenta onto a baking tray and smooth out using the back of a spoon. Leave to cool (this may take a few hours).

When nearly ready to serve, cut the polenta into pieces, of whatever shape or size you like, and dip them into the maize meal. Heat a little oil in a frying pan and fry the chips for a few minutes on each side, until they are a golden brown colour and crispy.

sea salt
230g polenta
2–3 tbsp maize meal
sesame or sunflower oil (for frying)

Sushi

250g sushi rice
10 sheets of nori
1 tbsp tahini (sesame seed paste)
1 tbsp umeboshi paste
1–2 tbsp sauerkraut
30g carrots, cut into long matchsticks
1 tsp wasabi powder
shoyu, to taste
pickled ginger slices, to serve

Cook the rice according to the packet instructions, then leave to one side to cool down.

Lay a sheet of nori, rough side up, on a sushi mat or any other flat surface. Dip a spatula into a jug of water and use it to spread some rice over the nori. Each time you add more rice, dip the spatula into the jug of water to stop the rice from sticking to it. Then spread the rice with a little tahini, a tiny amount of umeboshi paste and a little sauerkraut. Lay a few carrot matchsticks down the centre and, using the mat as a guide, roll up the sushi as if making a Swiss roll. Use a wet knife to cut it into eight slices.

Repeat as above with the remaining ingredients.

To make wasabi paste in which to dip the sushi, put the wasabi powder in a small dish and add a little water at a time. If you add too much water, you will need to add more wasabi. When you have got a thick paste, divide it between the serving plates. Spoon a little shoyu onto each plate too. Serve the sushi with a few slices of pickled ginger.

Nori seaweed is dried and sold in sheet form. It is the traditional Japanese wrapping for sushi, and is used in strips as a garnish on many dishes. The best quality nori is a glossy black-purple colour; after toasting it should turn a beautiful green.

This recipe makes about 80 rolls, which will serve 4 as a main course in my hungry household but is probably enough for 6 people.

Tempura Noodle Sushi

750g udon noodles (wheat)

4 sheets of nori

40g carrots, cut into long matchsticks

sunflower or sesame seed oil for deep-frying

FOR THE DIPPING SAUCE

2 tbsp shoyu

1 tbsp mirin

1 tsp water

2 tsp grated fresh ginger

Cook the noodles according to the packet directions. Divide the noodles into 4 portions.

Put a sheet of nori, rough side up, on a sushi mat or any other flat surface. Lay a quarter of the noodles in long rows across the nori. Put a quarter of the carrot matchsticks on top of the noodles. Using the mat as a guide, roll up the sushi as if making a Swiss roll. Press the roll firmly so the noodles stick to the nori. Cut each roll in half with a moistened knife. Repeat as above with the remaining ingredients.

Fill a deep-fat fryer or large saucepan with sufficient oil for deep-frying and heat. When the oil is ready (a cube of bread will brown in 30 seconds), deep-fry a few sushi for 3–5 minutes until a light golden brown. Remove using a slotted spoon and drain on a cake rack. Keep the sushi warm in the oven at 180°C/gas 4 while you cook the remaining sushi.

Prepare the sauce. Mix all the ingredients together and divide into 4 little dishes.

Cut the sushi into bite-sized pieces and serve with the dipping sauce.

Ginger is a root vegetable with a very pungent taste. To use fresh ginger in this recipe, peel it first and then grate it as finely as you can.

Garlic Rice

Heat the oil in a stainless steel wok (or large frying pan). Add the ginger and garlic, stirring constantly. Then add the cooked rice and stir very fast with a long wooden spatula for a few minutes.

The heat should be high but you must not let the ingredients burn. Add the salt and stir for another couple of minutes.

Switch off the heat and transfer the mixture to a serving dish. Add the parsley for decoration. This recipe is ideal for a quick lunch, served with some home-made pickles and a pressed salad (see page 70).

1–2 tsp olive or sesame oil

**5-cm piece of ginger,
very finely chopped**

**2–3 cloves of garlic, very finely
chopped**

**1 cup of short grain organic rice
(pre-cooked, either boiled
or pressure cooked)**

sea salt

**parsley, finely chopped,
for decoration**

Salt Sticks If you're using a pair of chopsticks to stir the rice, give it a quick stir then dip them in the salt, which will stick to them. A couple of dips and you should have added the right amount to your stir fry.

The Japanese Feng Shui expert Takashi Yoshikawa taught me how to cook this dish when he visited our house in London. As he stood over the hot wok, stirring its contents, he told me you have to sweat to really make this dish work. When he chopped the garlic and ginger I could hardly believe what tiny shreds he created. They were as thin as sewing threads.

Deep-fried Rice Balls

450g short-grain brown rice
50g sweet brown rice
½ tsp sea salt
4 tbsp sesame seeds
(brown or black)
sunflower oil (for deep-frying)

FOR THE DIPPING SAUCE
2 tbsp shoyu
2 tbsp water
1 tbsp brown rice vinegar
1-cm piece ginger, finely grated
2-cm piece daikon, finely grated

Brown rice vinegar is a mellow Japanese seasoning. The best varieties are made with nothing but spring water and organically grown brown rice.

Prepare the rice a few hours in advance. Mix the short-grain and sweet brown rice together. Wash and rinse the rice a few times, and transfer to a pressure cooker. Fill a large jug with water. Top the pan up with water using the following method: place the pressure cooker on a flat surface, put one hand inside, and rest the palm of your hand on the rice. Pour in water until it reaches your wrist. Leave the rice to soak for a few hours or overnight.

When ready to cook, add the salt then put the lid of the pressure cooker on tight and bring the rice to the boil. Make sure you do this slowly (medium heat is best), to avoid burning it. Place a flame diffuser on another ring, warm it up and when the pressure valve pops up, put the pan on the diffuser. Using a timer, cook the rice for 40 minutes from the moment the pressure valve comes up. When finished, switch off the cooker and remove from the diffuser. As soon as the pressure valve comes down, remove the lid and transfer the rice to a bowl. By removing the rice straight away you stop it from cooking further. Leave the rice to cool for a few hours.

Wet your hands, pick up a handful of rice and form a ball. Repeat, wetting your hands each time you do so to prevent the rice sticking to them. Place the balls in one bowl and the sesame seeds in another.

Add sufficient oil to a deep-fat fryer or saucepan and heat. The oil is hot enough when a grain of rice pops up to the surface within a few seconds of dropping it in. Coat each rice ball with sesame seeds and fry for a couple of minutes. Place a couple of sheets of kitchen roll on a large plate. Remove the rice balls using a slotted spoon and drain on the kitchen roll.

Mix all the sauce ingredients together and divide between 4 individual small dishes. Serve the rice balls with the dipping sauce.

Crunchy Filo Parcels

Preheat the oven to 200°C /gas 6.

Heat the oil in a large deep frying pan and stir in the onions. Add a dash of salt. This brings out the sweetness of the onions. Cook the onions, stirring occasionally, until softened (about 2–4 minutes).

Squeeze the tofu over the pan until it crumbles. Add 1 tbsp of the sparkling water and about 1½ tsp salt and mix well. Simmer on a medium to high heat until all the water has evaporated. Add the grated carrot. Mix it all in for a minute and remove the pan from the heat.

Unroll one sheet of filo pastry onto a clean surface. Add a few drops of the oil and rub it into the pastry with your fingers. Cover with another sheet of filo and a little more oil. Continue until you have 5 sheets of filo layered on top of each other. Spoon a fifth of the tofu filling into the centre and roll the pastry up like a Swiss roll. Transfer to a baking sheet. Repeat with the rest of the filo sheets and the filling. You should end up with 5 rolls.

Drizzle with a little sunflower oil and rub in with your fingers (this stops the filo from drying). Bake in the preheated oven for 20 minutes or until golden.

Sprinkle with a little of the remaining mineral water, turn the oven off and leave the parcels in the oven for 2–3 minutes. Take them out, sprinkle with a little more sparkling water and cover with a clean tea towel. (If you prefer your parcels crunchier, omit this step.)

Leave to sit for 10–15 minutes. Cut into 10-cm pieces, and serve.

1 tbsp organic sunflower oil
2 medium onions cut in half moons
sea salt
2 packets of organic tofu, drained
2 tbsp sparkling mineral water
1 large organic carrot, scrubbed and coarsely grated
approximately 350g filo pastry

filo pastry

Exciting Extras

Exciting Extras

In macrobiotics, a meal is not considered a meal unless it contains one grain and at least one vegetable dish. By this I mean vegetables of your choice (from broccoli or watercress to carrots, parsnip, kale, cabbage... the list is endless) cooked in any of a huge variety of ways – boiled, blanched, steamed, sautéed, baked, pressed and so on. A lot of people think that salad is sufficient or that tomatoes will do (remember tomato is a fruit). Everyone knows the importance of vegetables in the diet, but I am always amazed at how limited the average intake of vegetables is. Most people I know eat only one or two types, like carrots or frozen peas, and if I point this out they get very defensive.

Sadly, certain vegetables tend to be cooked during festive times only. For example, parsnips just make an appearance at Christmas in many households, which is a shame because

their natural sweetness is so calming for the body and helps with sugar cravings. As a child I always had vegetables with my main meals (in fact, the dinner ladies at school thought I was a weirdo because I went back for more cabbage), but I now include them at breakfast. Friends are shocked and horrified when they see

Find this delicious Pepper and Tomato Salad on page 75.

me munching on a carrot or a sprig of broccoli with my porridge. It's probably one of the hardest aspects of macrobiotics to grasp. Even if you have to have toast for breakfast you should try adding a vegetable.

If I feel a cold coming on, I indulge in mountains of rich green vegetables – I find them more effective than vitamins. When Drags and I are in the supermarket we get strange looks because our trolleys are loaded up with veggies. Small surprise that we are fully paid up members of the Green Party !

Tempura

sunflower or safflower oil
for deep-frying

150g cauliflower, cut into florets

75g carrots, half cut into
matchsticks and half
sliced diagonally

30g spring onions, halved

FOR THE BATTER

50g organic white unbleached
flour

¼ tsp sea salt

150ml cold sparkling water

FOR THE DIPPING SAUCE

2 tbsp shoyu

1 tbsp mirin (Japanese sweet
rice wine)

1 tsp brown rice vinegar

2-cm piece daikon, very
finely grated

pickles, to serve

Mix the flour and salt first and then stir in the water, the colder the water the better. Don't worry about lumps; there should be some.

Heat enough oil in a deep-fat fryer or deep saucepan. The oil is ready for cooking when a drop of batter added to the oil sinks to the bottom of the pan and immediately rises back to the surface.

Dip the vegetable pieces (one at a time) in the batter mixture and deep-fry for 3–4 minutes or until golden. Because the batter does not contain any eggs it will not turn very yellow. Drain the vegetables on a rack while you cook the rest. Skim the surface of the oil occasionally to keep it clean.

Mix all the dipping sauce ingredients together and place in individual small dishes. Serve tempura immediately – it is best eaten hot – with some pickles (said to be good for digesting oily foods).

Mirin is a sweet cooking wine, made from rice, water and a natural rice culture called koji. It sweetens and mellows the dipping sauce in this dish; brown rice vinegar and shoyu can be too strong on their own.

For successful tempura, you must make sure that all the ingredients are fresh, that you use a very good quality oil, that the batter is lumpy, and that the frying temperature is constant.

Deep-fried Burdock and Sauerkraut

50g flour

pinch of sea salt

50ml cold sparkling water or beer

5g kuzu diluted in 1 tbsp water

sesame oil (for deep frying)

100g burdock (unpeeled but washed thoroughly with a vegetable brush), cut into 5-cm pieces and then quartered

130g ready-made sauerkraut, finely chopped and any excess liquid squeezed out

1 tsp shoyu

Place the flour, sea salt, sparkling water or beer and kuzu in a mixing bowl and combine to form a batter. Make sure there are no lumps.

In a deep-fat fryer or deep saucepan, heat the oil. To test if it is hot enough, put in one drop of batter; it should spring back to the surface almost immediately.

Dip each piece of burdock in batter and deep-fry a few pieces at a time for 2–3 minutes or until crispy. Because there are no eggs in the batter, the pieces will not turn particularly yellow.

Meanwhile, place the sauerkraut in a 2-litre saucepan. As the burdock pieces are cooked, place them on top of the sauerkraut. Add 50ml cold water by pouring it down the side of the pan. Cover, place over a high heat and steam for 2 minutes. Season with shoyu and turn the heat off. Leave to stand for a couple of minutes before serving.

Burdock root (known in Japanese as gobo) is brown, thin and very long (usually 45–60cm). The skin has the best flavour, so don't peel the root – though you will need to clean it well. Prepared in this way, it imparts an earthy and energising quality.

Nishime

Place the kombu into a large heavy-based saucepan and then layer the vegetables on top.

Carefully add 400ml cold water so that you do not 'disturb' the vegetables. Sprinkle over a pinch of sea salt, cover and bring to the boil. Reduce the heat to medium and cook for 20–30 minutes. The water should reduce to about 5mm. Season with shoyu, replace the lid and simmer for another minute before serving.

10-cm piece kombu

1 medium onion, peeled and cut into quarters

150g pumpkin, scrubbed but unpeeled, cut into big chunks

150g carrots, scrubbed and cut into chunks

150g daikon, scrubbed and cut into chunks

pinch sea salt

1 tsp shoyu

When you're making a nishime dish, the vegetables are chunky and hearty and cooked for a long period of time so they're soft, rich and sweet but not mushy and tasteless.

Nishime is a cooking method whereby roots and round vegetables are combined and steamed together with a small amount of kombu and water. This particular cooking method is very good for deep nourishment and relaxing the digestive system.

Pickled Vegetables with Arame

250ml organic white wine vinegar
100ml brown rice syrup
1 tsp sea salt
1 tsp shoyu
70g daikon, cut into matchsticks
**70g carrots, washed and
cut into matchsticks**
**150g cucumber, cut
into matchsticks**
**1 bunch fresh flat-leaf parsley,
finely chopped**
3-cm piece ginger, grated
2 tbsp sesame oil
**1 small onion, cut into
half moons**
**20g arame sea vegetable,
pre-soaked in 100ml water for
10–15 minutes**
3 tbsp black sesame seeds

Bring 500ml cold water, the vinegar, rice syrup, sea salt and shoyu to the boil. Simmer for 2 minutes. Fill a 1-litre preserving jar with very hot water and leave for 5 minutes. Pour the water out and layer the vegetables in the following order: daikon, carrot and cucumber, placing some chopped parsley and ginger after each layer, ending with just parsley.

Pour the vinegar and rice syrup liquid over the vegetables and seal the jar. Leave to cool and then refrigerate. It should be ready in 2–3 days.

When ready to serve, heat the sesame oil in a heavy-based frying pan and sauté the onions for a few minutes over a medium to high heat. Add the arame and sauté for another minute. Add the soaking water from the vegetables and cook for 10–15 minutes over a medium heat or until the water has evaporated. Transfer to a bowl and leave the arame mixture to cool down. To dry-fry the sesame seeds, heat a frying pan over a high heat, add the seeds and toast for 3–5 minutes. Stir the pickled vegetables into the onion and arame mixture, then top with toasted sesame seeds.

Arame is a brown sea vegetable that grows in deep waters. It comes in thin, dried strips that expand on soaking or cooking. Because of its mild flavour, arame is probably the best sea vegetable to serve to someone who hasn't sampled this kind of delicacy before.

Kimpira

Heat the oil in a heavy-based saucepan. Sauté the burdock for 2 minutes. Add the carrots and sauté for 1 minute. Add the mirin and 50ml cold water. Cover and simmer on a medium to high heat for about 10 minutes, checking occasionally that there is enough water. Add the shoyu and simmer for another minute. Switch the heat off and add the shichimi. Leave to stand, covered, for a couple of minutes then serve with sprinkled sesame seeds.

1 tsp toasted sesame oil

100g burdock (gently scrubbed but unpeeled), cut into thin shavings or matchsticks

100g carrots, cut into thin shavings with a sharp knife

1 tbsp mirin (optional)

1 tbsp shoyu

¼ tsp shichimi

1 tsp black sesame seeds, dry-fried (see page 64)

Shichimi is a combination of seven dried and ground spices. Hot and spicy, it adds a gentle kick to this dish.

You can cut the vegetables in matchsticks for this dish, however they should be very, very fine. I have watched our friend Mr Yoshikawa cut them on a few occasions in my house. They were no thinner than a cotton thread. Unbelievable! Although I have made this dish many a time, I am still a long way from that perfection.

Fried Broccoli with Ginger and Garlic

Heat the oil in a deep frying pan (about 6cm deep). Stir in the garlic and ginger. Sauté for a minute or two on a high heat, then add the broccoli, chilli pepper flakes and 50ml cold water. Keep stirring for 5–10 minutes until the broccoli is cooked but still crunchy (it should have a lovely deep green colour – but don't overcook it). Add the salt and sauté for another minute. Transfer to a serving dish and eat while still warm.

2 tbsp olive oil
1 medium clove garlic, halved
2-cm piece ginger, thinly sliced
250g broccoli, cut into medium-sized florets
¼ tsp chilli pepper flakes
½ tsp sea salt

Runner Beans with Miso Dressing

Heat up a large frying pan and add the sesame oil. Fry the runner beans whole in the hot oil for about 5 minutes, stirring continuously.

Mix the miso paste with 50ml cold water and pour the liquid over the beans. Cover the pan with the lid and turn off the heat. Leave for a minute or two for the flavours to infuse, then serve immediately.

1 tbsp sesame oil
250g runner beans, washed and trimmed
1 tbsp organic barley miso

Nutty Carrot Mash

500g carrots
pinch of sea salt
1 tsp hazelnut butter (available in jars, like peanut butter)
1 tsp brown rice vinegar

Place the carrots in a heavy-based saucepan and add 500ml cold water. Cover, bring to a boil, then add the salt. Simmer, covered, over a medium to high heat for about 20–30 minutes. Keep checking the water. When there is only about 1cm water left, turn off heat. Place the carrots, the remaining water and the hazelnut butter in a blender and process until smooth. Before serving, transfer to a bowl and stir in the brown rice vinegar.

Steamed Carrots with Tahini Dressing

150g thin carrots, preferably with green tops
1 tbsp tahini
½ tsp umeboshi paste
1 tsp shoyu
½ tsp brown rice vinegar

Heat 50ml cold water in the base of a steamer. Place the whole carrots in the top part of the steamer and place it on top of the base. Steam for approximately 5–7 minutes or until the carrots are tender.

Meanwhile, prepare the dressing. Mix together the tahini, umeboshi paste, shoyu and brown rice vinegar. You may need to add a small amount of cold water if the mixture is too thick.

Place the carrots in a serving dish and pour the dressing across the middle. Serve immediately.

Tahini is a paste made from raw, peeled sesame seeds. It is quite rich and oily, so don't add too much to this dish.

Chinese Cabbage and Sauerkraut Rolls

4 large Chinese cabbage leaves
4 tbsp ready-made sauerkraut

In a large saucepan, bring 1 litre cold water to the boil, covered. Remove the lid and blanch the cabbage leaves, one at a time, for approximately 30 seconds (the whole leaf should be in the water). Allow the leaves to cool.

Place the leaves on a flat surface with the inner part facing upwards. In the middle of each leaf, put 1 tbsp sauerkraut, then roll up the leaf starting from the stem end.

Squeeze each gently to get rid of any excess liquid, and serve immediately.

chinese cabbage

Green Salad with Tofu Dressing

To blanch the tofu, half fill a 1-litre saucepan with water, and bring the water to a boil. Drop the tofu in and allow to cook for 2–3 minutes. Remove with a slotted spoon and mash it up in a blender. Add the tahini, umeboshi paste, vinegar and 4 tbsp water and blend into a fine, smooth paste. Toss with the iceberg and rocket leaves, and serve. Alternatively, you can serve the dressing on the side.

350g iceberg lettuce, torn into small pieces
50g rocket leaves, torn into small pieces

FOR THE DRESSING
100g fresh tofu
1 tsp tahini
½ tsp umeboshi paste
2 tsp brown rice vinegar

Pressed Cucumber, Chinese Cabbage and Radish Salad

150g cucumber, cut in half then thinly sliced
200g Chinese cabbage, finely sliced
100g radishes, thinly sliced diagonally
¼ tsp sea salt

Place the cucumber, cabbage and radishes in a deep bowl; sprinkle over the salt and mix gently with your hands for a minute. Put a flat plate on top of the ingredients, within the bowl, and weigh it down with a 1kg weight. Leave for 10–15 minutes.

Remove the weight and, holding the plate firmly in place, drain the liquid from the vegetables over a sink. Place the pressed ingredients in a serving bowl and serve.

Other vegetables that you can use to make a delicious pressed salad are grated carrots, grated or finely chopped daikon, shredded white cabbage, watercress and parsley.

This salad is very refreshing and delicious as it is, but if you like, you can season it with a dressing of your choice before serving. I usually sprinkle over 1 tbsp of pan-roasted sunflower seeds too.

Chinese cabbage is greenish-white in colour. It should be crunchy for this salad, so don't press it for too long or it will wilt.

Wakame and Cucumber Salad

Place the cucumber slices in a deep bowl. Put a flat plate on top and weigh it down with a 1kg weight. Leave for 10–15 minutes.

Remove the weight and, holding the plate firmly in place, drain the liquid from the cucumber over a sink.

Place the wakame in a small bowl and cover with cold water. Leave to soak for 5 minutes. Remove, reserving the soaking water, and chop the wakame into small pieces. Place 5ml of the soaking water into a small pan over a medium heat. Add the wakame and simmer for a few minutes until all the water evaporates. Then add the miso, diluted with 1 tbsp cold water, and turn the heat off. Take the wakame out of the pan and leave it to cool before mixing it with the cucumber. Finally, add the spring onions and serve.

200g cucumber (peeled, if not organic), and cut into crescent slices
1 piece dried wakame, 8 x 2-cm
1 tsp sweet miso
1 small spring onion, finely chopped diagonally

Wakame is an edible sea vegetable, rich in minerals and protein. It looks similar to kombu, but is much softer, and combines beautifully with miso. Usually it comes in strips, but occasionally you can find it already crumbled.

Blanched Salad with Tofu Mayonnaise

50g cabbage, cut
into 2-cm squares

50g carrots, cut diagonally
into 5-mm pieces

50g broccoli, cut into
small florets

50g cauliflower,
cut into small florets

50g spring greens, cut
into 1-cm slices

FOR THE TOFU MAYONNAISE

250g tofu, steamed for
2–3 minutes and left to cool

4 tbsp sesame oil

2 tbsp brown rice vinegar

1 tbsp lemon juice

1 tbsp barley miso

½ tsp sea salt

Place 2 litres water in a large saucepan and bring to the boil, covered, over a medium heat. Remove the lid, turn the heat up to high, and add the cabbage. Blanch for 1 minute. Remove using a slotted spoon and place on a plate.

Repeat with the carrots, broccoli, cauliflower and spring greens. Allow the vegetables to cool.

Meanwhile, prepare the tofu mayonnaise. Put all the ingredients in a blender or food processor and process until smooth.

To serve, place the cooled vegetables in a serving dish and pour the mayonnaise over.

Blanched vegetables should be bright and crispy. Soft greens such as parsley or watercress are usually boiled for less than a minute, but other types of vegetable take a little longer. When the colour of the vegetables intensifies, they are ready. You should time the blanching from when you put the vegetables in the pan – don't wait for the water to reboil.

Watercress and Shiitake Salad

2 tbsp pumpkin seeds, washed
1 tbsp olive oil
150g fresh shiitake mushrooms, sliced
200g watercress, washed and cut
into similar lengths as the shiitake
1 tbsp shoyu

Toast the pumpkin seeds: brush a frying pan with the olive oil and heat the seeds over a medium heat; stir frequently to prevent burning. Cook until light brown all over. Place the seeds on a plate to cool.

Pour in just enough water to cover the surface of the frying pan. Heat the water and add the mushrooms. Sauté for 1–2 minutes. Add the watercress and cook for another 1–2 minutes, stirring occasionally. Season with shoyu and transfer to a serving bowl. Mix in the pumpkin seeds before serving.

Don't be tempted to use dried shiitake mushrooms for this recipe: the fresh ones work much better as their woody, fruity flavour perfectly complements the strong-tasting watercress and crunchy pumpkin seeds. The quick cooking method in this recipe allows the mushrooms to retain their texture.

Pepper and Tomato Salad

350g long green peppers
olive oil (for frying)
sea salt
1 large clove garlic, crushed
200g tomatoes, chopped finely
fresh flat-leaf parsley, for
decoration

Preheat the oven to 200°C/gas 6. Place the peppers in a roasting tin and bake, turning once, for 10–12 minutes or until the skin is charred. Transfer the peppers to a deep dish and then wrap the dish with a large cotton tea towel to allow the peppers to 'sweat'. Leave for an hour or so.

Using your fingers, peel the peppers but do not remove the stalks or the seeds. Fry the peppers on each side in a little oil and sprinkle with sea salt. Remove from the pan and place in a serving bowl.

Into the same frying pan, add a further 1 tsp oil and fry the garlic until golden. Add the tomatoes and 150ml cold water and simmer over a medium to high heat for 5 minutes. Season with ¼ tsp sea salt.

Pour the tomato mixture over the peppers and garnish with the parsley.

flat-leaf parsley

Tofu and Green Pepper Salad

600g green peppers
250g tofu
2 tbsp sunflower oil
1 tbsp balsamic or white wine vinegar
1 small clove garlic, crushed
½ tsp sea salt
flat-leaf parsley, for decoration

This dish can be made a day in advance – it tastes even better if the peppers and tofu soak up the dressing overnight.

Preheat the oven to 200°C/gas 6. Place the peppers in a roasting tin and bake, turning once, for 10–12 minutes or until the skin is charred. Transfer the peppers to a deep dish and then wrap the dish with a large cotton tea towel to allow the peppers to 'sweat'. Leave for an hour or so.

Using your fingers, remove the stalks, skin and seeds from the peppers, and cut them into strips. Place in a serving bowl.

Bring 150ml water to the boil in a medium saucepan and blanch the tofu for 2–3 minutes. Drain and leave to cool. Cut the tofu into 3-cm long, thick matchsticks. Add to the peppers.

In a small dish, mix the oil, vinegar, 1 tbsp cold water, garlic and salt. Pour over the tofu and peppers and refrigerate for 30 minutes. Serve garnished with the flat-leaf parsley.

Roasting peppers always seemed rather a palaver, and for years I avoided it. But it's really just a case of shoving them in a hot oven, under a grill or on a barbecue and giving them an occasional twirl. Mixed with lightly steamed tofu and seasoned with garlic, this is a very satisfying summer salad.

Tofu and Cucumber Salad

250g tofu
1 small cucumber (preferably organic)
2½ tsp white wine vinegar (preferably organic)
1 tsp shoyu
½ tsp sea salt
1 tsp rice syrup
1 tsp sesame oil
1 tsp black sesame seeds, toasted (see page 64)
½ tsp Thai (or any other) spicy green curry paste

With a cool and refreshing taste, this dish is ideal for summer.

Pour 1 litre water into the base of a steamer, bring to the boil and steam the tofu for 3–4 minutes. Drain and cool. Cut the cooked tofu into 2-cm cubes.

Halve the cucumber lengthwise and remove the seeds from the middle with a small spoon. Cut in half again. Cut off the ends and peel, if it is not organic. Cut the cucumber into 1-cm pieces and mix with the tofu. Place in a serving bowl. Mix all the remaining ingredients together and pour over the cucumber and tofu. Leave to marinate for an hour before serving.

Thai curry paste is a mixture of various spices: it is very hot so use sparingly! It can be either green or red (depending on the colour of the chillies used), so be sure to use the green variety.

Potato and Watercress Salad

Bring 1½ litres cold water to the boil. Add the potatoes and cook until soft (about 15 minutes). Add the watercress and cook for another 5 minutes. Drain and place in a serving bowl.

Mash the vegetables with a fork and then add all the dressing ingredients to the bowl. Refrigerate for several hours or until completely cold. Serve garnished with the coriander.

700g white potatoes, peeled and cut into 3-cm cubes

100g watercress, cut into 2-cm lengths

fresh coriander leaves, for decoration

FOR THE DRESSING
1¼ tsp sea salt

1 tbsp sunflower oil

1½ tbsp white wine vinegar (preferably organic)

Quickly Pickled Radishes

Cut the ends off and finely slice the radishes, then place them on a deep flat bowl. In a small saucepan, add the vinegar to 160ml water and bring the mixture to the boil. Remove from the heat and pour over the radishes. Leave for 10 minutes.

Drain and reserve the vinegar mixture and place the radishes on a serving dish. Refrigerate the vinegar and use later in salad dressings or other recipes.

150g radishes
100ml umeboshi vinegar

Delicious Desserts

Delicious Desserts

put some sweetness in your life

Everyone needs a bit of sweetness in their lives and a life without desserts would be a dull one. There are times, especially when I am in New York, when I still indulge in cheese cakes, or the occasional cream brulée. But through macrobiotics I have discovered how to create sweet and delicious puddings without using sugar.

To many people, a dessert means something crammed with sugar and cream, or served with a big dollop of sweet chocolate sauce or custard on the top. Making macrobiotic puddings – without processed sugar, cream, milk, butter and eggs – might therefore seem rather daunting, but they are really very easy to make once you've got the hang of some of the many delicious ingredients at your disposal.

I've proudly mastered Drags' sugar-free apple crumble. When I make it for friends, they are shocked by how sweet it is. For me, one of the most exciting and challenging aspects of cooking is to take a traditional dessert and adapt it to macro style. Soy is a great substitute for dairy products, and with soy milk, cream and yogurt you can create a huge range of mouth-watering puddings. And instead of sugar, try using naturally sweet ingredients such as fruits (fresh and dried) or grain syrups.

Desserts full of processed sugar can be instantly gratifying, but those sweetened with grain syrups such as rice, millet, corn and barley have a much longer-lasting effect. To give an analogy, it is like chucking newspaper into a fire as opposed to coal, which burns more slowly and keeps its heat for longer. Sweetness is very important in our diets, and if I don't have good-quality desserts like the afore-mentioned crumble, or Amasake Mousse, I go off the edge and eat doughnuts. As my friend Amanda says, 'It is not enough to have a cake – you've got to fry it too'.

If macro desserts frighten you, experiment first with dishes like Coffee Mousse, which is very quick and easy to make and leaves you feeling like a culinary mastermind.

Glazed Kuzu Pears

2 large or 4 small pears, halved
125ml pear or apple juice
pinch of sea salt
4 tsp maple syrup

FOR THE MARZIPAN
30–40g ground almonds
1 tbsp rice syrup

FOR THE SAUCE
1 tbsp kuzu powder
1 tbsp lemon juice
1 tsp lemon zest

Place the pears with the cut side up and the pear juice in a pan. Bring to the boil. Reduce the heat to medium. Add a pinch of sea salt, and cook for 5–7 minutes. Remove the pears using a slotted spoon and reserve the cooking liquid. Place half a pear (or two small halves) in each serving bowl with 1 tsp maple syrup.

Prepare the marzipan. Heat up a frying pan and dry-fry the almonds for 3–5 minutes, stirring constantly to prevent the almonds from burning. When they are golden brown, remove from the heat. Heat the rice syrup and add the roasted ground almonds. Mix and stir until the mixture thickens. Place one-quarter of the marzipan in the hollow of each pear half.

In a small saucepan, mix together the reserved pear juice and the kuzu powder. Heat, stirring constantly, for 3–5 minutes until the kuzu thickens. Stir in the lemon juice and zest and pour the sauce over the pears to serve.

Kuzu (also known as kudzu) is a white starch made from the root of the kuzu plant. Here it is used to thicken the glaze – it is a healthy alternative to cornflour.

Peach and Apple Tango

1 litre peach and apple juice
pinch of sea salt
4 tbsp kanten or agar agar flakes
**4 sugar-free waffle biscuits
(or any other sugar-free,
good-quality biscuit)**
**1 tbsp ready-made hazelnut
or almond butter**
chopped almonds, for decoration

Prepare at least 4 hours ahead. Place the juice in a pan with a pinch of sea salt. Add the kanten or agar agar flakes and bring to the boil. Simmer for 10–15 minutes over a medium heat.

Put the waffle biscuits in a deep, flat dish and pour the hot juice over. Leave to cool for a while and then refrigerate for 2–3 hours or until set.

Put 1 tbsp of either hazelnut or almond butter in a blender and add the juice and biscuit mixture. Blend them all together. Serve the dessert in small dishes, garnished with some chopped almonds.

Waffle biscuits are all natural, and made without any sugar. They give this dessert a slightly biscuity flavour and richer texture.

Nutty Strudels

Preheat the oven to 200°C/gas 6.

In a mixing bowl, mix the apples, maple syrup, walnuts, raisins and breadcrumbs together. Unroll 4 sheets of filo pastry. Put 1 sheet on the worktop, sprinkle with a few drops of corn oil and brush it all over the pastry. Cover with another piece of filo and a little more oil. Continue until you have used all 4 sheets. Put 3 or 4 tablespoons of the apple filling in the centre of the pastry and roll up like a Swiss roll. Repeat until you have used up all the filo and the filling.

Place the rolls on a baking tray. Drizzle with some more oil and bake for about 20–25 minutes. Turn the oven off. Take the rolls out of the oven and sprinkle with mineral water (this stops the pastry from drying out). Put the rolls back in the oven, without turning it on again, and leave the rolls in the oven for 5 minutes. Cut them into 10-cm pieces and serve. These are delicious served with some sugar-free vanilla soy dessert.

**MAKES ABOUT 16
INDIVIDUAL STRUDELS**

**600g eating apples, peeled
and grated**

3 tbsp maple syrup

**100g walnuts, lightly roasted
and ground**

**50g raisins, washed and soaked in
hot water for 10 minutes**

1 tbsp wholemeal breadcrumbs

400g fresh filo pastry

2 tbsp corn oil

3–4 tbsp sparkling mineral water

vanilla soy dessert (optional)

Desserts were always something I had the horrors about because they are usually so fattening. This dish is sweetened with maple syrup, but if the apples are sweet enough you don't need to add any sweetener. The combination of sweet apples, nuts and flaky pastry is simply stupendous!

Amasake Mousse

370g amasake
1 tbsp kuzu powder
100g roasted ground almonds
2 tbsp freshly squeezed orange juice
flaked almonds, for decoration

Place the amasake and 100ml cold water in a small saucepan. Measure a further 100ml cold water into a jug and stir in the kuzu powder. Pour the kuzu mixture into the amasake and slowly bring to a boil, stirring constantly. Just before the kuzu starts to thicken, add the almonds. Turn off the heat and stir in the orange juice.

This mousse is delicious warm or at room temperature. Serve garnished with a few flaked almonds.

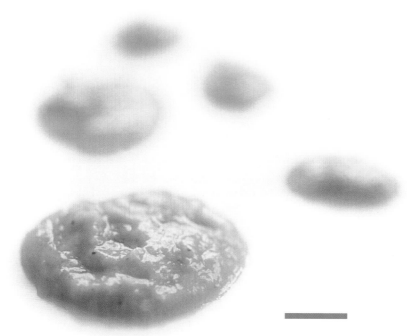

Amasake is a natural sweetener made from cooked sweet brown rice and koji starter.

Strawberry Parcels

Place the flours, oats and salt in a mixing bowl. Stir in 80ml hot water and mix to form a dough. Sprinkle some extra flour on the work surface. Roll out the pastry to a 5mm thickness. Cut the pastry into twenty 6 x 4-cm rectangles. Put a strawberry quarter on one side of the pastry, dampen the edges of the pastry with water and fold the pastry over to make a 3 x 4-cm panel. Seal the edges together. Repeat with the remaining pastry and strawberry quarters.

Heat enough oil in a deep-fat fryer or saucepan to deep-fry the parcels. Test to see if the oil is hot enough by putting a tiny piece of pastry into the fat; if it rises straight to the top, the oil is ready. Fry a few parcels at a time, for 2–3 minutes or until golden. Cool on a wire rack lined with kitchen roll to absorb any excess oil. Cook the remaining parcels in the same way, checking that the oil is hot enough between batches. Use the 'soaking' maple syrup and the juice from the strawberries as a dipping sauce.

MAKES 20 PARCELS
3 tbsp wholemeal flour
3 tbsp unbleached white flour
6 tbsp porridge oats
pinch of sea salt
5 medium strawberries,
quartered and soaked in 5 tbsp
maple syrup for a few hours
safflower or sunflower oil for
deep-frying

One thing I never have a problem sampling is Dragana's sugar-free desserts. These strawberry parcels are like sweet samosas and are very yummy. The only problem is that they are so small you can easily get carried away and eat too many of them. Self-control is advised...

Jammy Tarts

MAKES 15–20 TARTS

300g 80% wholemeal flour (preferably organic)

¼ tsp sea salt

100ml corn oil

50ml maple syrup

4–6 tbsp sparkling mineral water (or enough to make a dough)

sugar-free jam of your choice

Preheat the oven to 200°C/gas 6.

Combine the flour and the sea salt in a mixing bowl. Mix the oil and the syrup in a jug and then add it to the flour. Slowly, add enough water to form a dough. Knead lightly for a minute with your hands. Try not to work the pastry too much or it will be tough: it should remain powdery. Put the pastry in the freezer for 5 minutes.

Remove the dough from the freezer. Spread a little flour over the worktop and gently roll out the dough to a thickness of about 7–8mm. Using a 4-cm round pastry cutter, stamp out 15 or so rounds. Place each pastry circle in a muffin tray, and make a little depression in the pastry with your thumb. Fill each with ½ tsp of jam.

Bake in the oven for 15–20 minutes.

Unlike my Granny's jam tarts, these ones are free of butter and sugar (not that I complained about my Granny's at the time!). Children love them, and seem to be able to knock them up with great ease.

Almond and Hazelnut Biscuits

MAKES 15–20 BISCUITS
60g almonds
60g hazelnuts
120g wholemeal flour
180g white unbleached flour
1 tbsp salt-free baking powder
50ml apple juice
100ml maple syrup
½ tsp vanilla essence
oil, for greasing
sugar-free jam (optional)

Preheat the oven to 200°C/gas 6.

Dry-roast the almonds and hazelnuts: place in a non-stick, heavy frying pan and stir over a low heat for 2–4 minutes until lightly toasted on all sides. Cool and roughly chop the roasted nuts.

Mix the flours and baking powder in a mixing bowl. Add the almonds and hazelnuts. In a blender, mix together the apple juice, maple syrup and vanilla essence. Pour over the flour mixture. Stir to form a smooth dough, adding more flour if necessary.

On a lightly floured worktop, roll out the dough to about 1cm thickness. Using biscuit cutters, cut out different shapes and place onto a lightly oiled baking tray. Bake for 15–20 minutes. If you've got a very sweet tooth, serve topped with some sugar-free jam.

Nutty Rice Pudding

Dry-roast the hazelnuts: place in a non-stick, heavy frying pan and stir over a low heat until lightly toasted on all sides. This should take 2–4 minutes. Roughly chop the roasted hazelnuts.

Mix the rice and rice milk together in a medium saucepan. Bring to the boil then reduce the heat to medium-low and simmer for 10–15 minutes. Add the raisins, hazelnuts, orange zest and juice. Simmer for another minute. Add the maple syrup and turn off the heat. Serve the pudding warm in individual bowls with a sprinkle of cinnamon.

100g hazelnuts

600g pre-cooked rice (70% short grain brown rice, 30% sweet brown rice), see page 54

600ml rice milk (vanilla flavour)

100g raisins, washed in warm water

1 medium orange (zest and juice)

3 tbsp maple syrup

ground cinnamon, for decoration

Rice milk is better for your digestion than soy milk, and is delicious in desserts. It comes in various flavours, but for this recipe I like to use the vanilla one.

Broken Biscuit Crumble

500g organic apples, peeled and coarsely chopped

500g organic pears, peeled and coarsely chopped

juice of 2 medium-sized organic oranges

60ml sugar-free peach jam

150ml maple syrup

400g Bio Malt sugar-free biscuits (or any other plain sugar-free biscuits)

50g flaked almonds

Preheat the oven to 180°C/gas 4.

Place the chopped apples and pears in an ovenproof dish. In a small mixing bowl, stir together the orange juice, jam and maple syrup and pour the mixture over the fruit.

Wrap the biscuits in a large cotton tea towel, and then crush them to fine crumbs with a rolling pin. Sprinkle the biscuit crumbs over the fruit and scatter the flaked almonds on top. Bake for 20–25 minutes.

This sugar-free crumble was the first dessert I learnt to make and it's delicious. Using apple juice and maple syrup and the natural sugar of the fruits, you discover that there is absolutely no need for any processed sugar. Crumble is such a traditional British dish and I have fond memories of it from my youth. It's one of those desserts that many people feel can only be made in the traditional way. Wrong. This version is just as yummy!

agar agar

Coffee Mousse

300ml organic sugar-free apple juice

5 tbsp instant yannoh coffee

4 tbsp agar agar

1 tsp natural vanilla essence

2 tbsp smooth organic peanut butter

3 tbsp corn and rice syrup

a few dry-roasted walnuts, finely chopped, for decoration

Place the apple juice with 150ml cold water in a 1-litre saucepan and bring to the boil. Put the yannoh in a cup, add a few tbsp water and mix to a smooth paste. Add the paste and agar agar flakes to the apple and water mixture, and stir well. Cook for 10 minutes on a medium heat until the agar agar completely dissolves. Turn off the heat and pour into a large dish. Leave to cool for 15 minutes and then refrigerate for about an hour or until the mixture has set.

Once set, put the mousse into a blender with the vanilla essence, peanut butter and syrup, and process until smooth. Spoon into 4 bowls and chill for 5 minutes. Decorate with a sprinkling of chopped walnuts.

Chestnut Balls

250g dried chestnuts

50g aduki beans

800ml sugar-free fruit juice (any kind you like)

100g raisins

150g dry roasted hazelnuts finely chopped

500g vanilla soy dessert

Place the chestnuts and beans in a large bowl, cover with the fruit juice and leave to soak overnight. Next day, put the contents of the bowl in a pressure cooker with the raisins and cook for 45 minutes. Turn the heat off, reduce the pressure slowly, uncover and leave to cool down. Use a slotted spoon to take the chestnuts out of the cooker. Remove any remaining skin, as this tends to be bitter. Put all the ingredients in a blender and process, or simply mash them with a fork. Form the mixture into spheres the size of golf balls with moistened hands – you should end up with about 12 balls. Roll these in the chopped hazelnuts, and serve with vanilla soy dessert.

Pancakes

Preheat the oven to 160°C/gas 3.

Mix the flour and sea salt together in a mixing bowl. Dilute the kuzu in a few tbsp beer or water and stir until it dissolves. Make a well in the middle and gradually add the kuzu and the rest of the beer or water, stirring constantly. When you have added 300ml of the liquid, the mixture should form a wet but firm dough. Pound with a wooden spoon for 5 minutes, making sure there are no lumps. Thin the batter down with the remaining water or beer and stir well. Leave it in the refrigerator for 15 minutes.

Stir 1 tbsp sunflower oil into the batter. Pour ¼ tsp oil into a medium-sized heavy-based frying pan and heat over a high heat. Pour in one ladleful of batter, swirling the pan as you pour, to ensure the base of the pan is covered with batter. Cook for 1–2 minutes until the batter is set and just starting to turn golden on the base. Flip the pancake over using a palette knife and cook the other side for 2 minutes. Repeat with the remaining batter to make about 20 pancakes. Keep them warm in the oven while you cook the remainder.

Serve the pancakes warm with your favourite jam, or maple syrup and lemon juice.

MAKES ABOUT 20 PANCAKES
250g 80% wholemeal flour (preferably organic)
pinch of sea salt
1 tsp kuzu powder
500ml Budweiser beer or cold sparkling mineral water
1 tbsp sunflower oil, plus extra for cooking

bg

These are easy to put together once you relinquish your fear of pancake-making! You really have to put some elbow into the batter, and also master how to ease each ladleful into the pan so that the batter evenly covers the base of the pan. Although the serving suggestion here is for making desserts, these pancakes are also delicious with savoury fillings.

Hunza Apricots with Vanilla Custard

32 hunza apricots
juice and rind of ½ lemon
1 tbsp arrowroot
500g vanilla soy dessert

Soak the apricots in 250ml cold water overnight. Place the apricots in a 1-litre saucepan with the soaking water, cover and bring to the boil. Reduce the heat to medium-low and simmer for about 15–20 minutes. Turn off the heat and leave to stand for 5 minutes.

Remove the apricots with a slotted spoon, then place 8 into each serving bowl. In a cup dilute the arrowroot with 1 tbsp cold water and add this to the reserved liquid in the saucepan. Turn the heat back to high and stir constantly for 2 minutes or until the liquid thickens. Turn off the heat and add the lemon juice and rind. Spoon the liquid over the apricots – there should be about 2 tbsp for each bowl. Finish with a few scoops of vanilla soy dessert on top.

Hunza apricots are best served in small portions, as they are extremely sweet and rich. One day I served my small army of children eight apricots each and they all agreed it was too much! They still managed to polish their bowls, though!!! Enjoy.

Stuffed Apples

Soak the raisins for 10–15 minutes in a small bowl of hot water. Wash the apples and de-core them with an apple corer or knife. Use a teaspoon to hollow out the centres of the apples further. Put the tahini and miso in a bowl and combine with a spoon. Next, stir in the raisins, cinnamon, walnuts and 1 tbsp of water. Stuff the apples with the mixture and then place them in a large, deep pan. Add 500ml water or 250ml water combined with 250ml apple juice, and cover the pan. Bring to the boil. Once boiling, reduce the heat to medium-low and steam the apples for 10–15 minutes or until the apples are soft but not mushy. Turn the heat off and remove the apples, reserving the cooking liquid in the pan. Place each apple in a serving bowl.

Make the glaze by diluting the kuzu with 1 tbsp of cold water, and adding it to the liquid in which the apples have been cooked. Gently heat the pan for 2–3 minutes until the kuzu has thickened, stirring constantly to prevent lumps of kuzu forming. Add the corn and rice syrup to the kuzu mixture, and pour an equal amount of glaze onto each of the apples.

6 medium size apples
1 tbsp barley miso
3 tbsp tahini
100g raisins
1 tsp cinnamon
50g oil-roasted walnuts, finely chopped
250ml apple juice (optional)

FOR THE GLAZE
1 tbsp kuzu
1 tbsp corn and rice syrup

I remember having stuffed baked apples regularly as a child – they make a very inexpensive and effective dessert. In today's world of cheesecakes and brulées, the hearty apple has been given the cold shoulder. But once you have tried this dish, you'll be amazed at how quick and easy it is to make and how naturally sweet and scrumptious it is.

Summer Fruits in Syrup

225g strawberries
150g raspberries
150g blackberries
125g blueberries
200ml strawberry and banana juice, freshly pressed
25ml rum
1 tbsp orange rind
1 tbsp maple syrup
1 tsp ginger, grated
fresh mint leaves, for decoration
soy cream (optional)

Wash all the fruits and place them loosely in a large bowl – be sure not to squash them. In a separate bowl, mix the juice, rum, orange rind, maple syrup and ginger, and then pour this mixture over the fruits. Leave to stand for a couple of hours to allow the flavourings to infuse the fruits. Serve garnished with mint leaves and soy cream if desired. I like to add a little more orange rind just before serving.

All summer fruits are delicious in this recipe, so if you can't obtain the particular ones I have suggested, do experiment with other types. You can also play around with the flavourings: add more orange, ginger or rum to taste.

Blissful Breakfasts

Blissful Breakfasts

carrots and cornflakes

Although Drags readily admits that she's not 'a breakfast person', I certainly am. When I was a kid, breakfast was usually porridge as there were six children in our household, or toast dripping with butter. When it comes to breakfast, most of us give ourselves limited choices. For a start, it's quite difficult to decide what you want to eat first thing in the morning. Certain foods say breakfast while others do not – I mean, you wouldn't rustle up a shepherdess pie first thing in the morning. But with macrobiotics, you really do have a variety of ingredients at your disposal.

I still have instant porridge oat flakes when I'm in a hurry, but using whole oats is much better. This takes longer, but Drags has come up with a cunning plan whereby you half cook them the night before. Instead of toast, I often have steamed sourdough bread which takes some getting used to after a life time of toast. Spreads like houmous or sugar-free jam can be a blissful way to start the day (but obviously not used together). The trick is to change what you have for breakfast every day. Fried Mochi, one of our breakfast recipes, is a very good alternative to fried bread, which is something my dad used to make on Sunday mornings. Mochi may look like cubes of plastic but don't be put off: it is quick to fry, and because it is made from pounded sweet brown rice, it is a good complex carbohydrate and will keep you going till lunch.

Scrambled tofu is one of my favourites for breakfast - I love it!

Don't forget to have at least one vegetable dish with whatever you munch on first thing in the morning. This does take some getting used to, but after a while it will all seem completely normal. Carrots, broccoli and cauliflower are probably easy choices to start with.

If you are stuck on traditional breakfast cereals, try organic sugar-free cornflakes with rice, soy and oat milk – or perhaps a squeeze of fresh orange or apple juice. Toasted sesame or sunflower seeds are delicious sprinkled on top.

Steamed Sourdough Bread with Tahini and Jam

8 slices of sourdough bread (rice, barley, rye or any other)
8 tsp light tahini
8 tsp sugar-free jam

Place 250ml water in a pan and bring to the boil. Position a bamboo steamer on top. Place the bread in the steamer, cover and leave for 3–4 minutes over a low heat. Remove the bread and place it on a serving plate. Spread evenly with tahini and top this with a layer of your favourite jam.

Make sure you choose the right size pan to fit the steamer, otherwise you will either have steam escaping in all directions or else risk setting the steamer on fire!

Steamed Sourdough Bread with Houmous and Sauerkraut

8 slices of sourdough bread (rice, barley, rye or any other)
250g ready-made houmous
8 tbsp natural sauerkraut

Place 250ml water in a pan. Cover, and bring to the boil. Remove the lid and position a wooden steamer on top. Place the bread in the steamer and cover. Leave for 3–4 minutes over a low heat. Turn off the heat, remove the bread and place it on a serving plate. Spread each slice with a generous layer of houmous and top with 1 tbsp sauerkraut.

Soft Rice with Umeboshi

600g cooked rice (see page 54)
10g umeboshi plum

Place the rice and plum with 600ml cold water in a 2-litre, covered saucepan and bring to the boil.

Reduce the heat and simmer semi-covered for 30–45 minutes. (Check after 30 minutes that there is still some water left.) Turn off the heat and leave to stand for another 5–10 minutes.

This dish is best eaten immediately and without decoration.

Although this dish takes about an hour to cook, it requires very little attention, which means that you can be getting ready for the day whilst it is cooking. This particular breakfast is very good if you suffer from any digestive problems, have lost your appetite or experience frequent tension in your stomach.

Fried Mochi with Syrup

maple syrup

Warm a cast-iron frying pan over a low heat for 1 minute. Add the oil, turn the heat up to medium and wait for half a minute. Add the mochi, cover and fry each side for 2–3 minutes until it puffs up slightly. Meanwhile, place the rice and maple syrups in a small pan and heat until they start to bubble. Take the mochi out of the frying pan, and put two blocks on each plate. Pour a small amount of the sauce on each serving of mochi whilst it is still hot. To serve, squeeze a few drops of lemon juice over the mochi.

8 blocks of mochi, cut in quarters
2–3 tbsp sesame or sunflower oil

FOR THE SAUCE
2 tbsp rice syrup
1 tbsp maple syrup
a few drops of lemon juice, freshly squeezed

Fried Mochi Savoury

Warm a cast-iron frying pan over a low heat for 1 minute. Add the oil, turn the heat up to medium and wait for half a minute. Add the mochi, cover and fry each side for 2–3 minutes. Take the mochi out and put 2 blocks on each plate. Mix all the dressing ingredients together and divide between servings, spreading it evenly on top of the mochi slices.

8 blocks of mochi
2–3 tbsp sesame or sunflower oil

FOR THE DRESSING
1 tbsp natural sauerkraut (consisting of just cabbage and salt), finely chopped
50g fresh daikon, finely grated
1 tsp shoyu
1 tsp brown rice vinegar
1 tbsp cold water
½ tsp nori flakes

Creamy Polenta with Syrup

150g organic polenta
maple syrup, to taste
50g sunflower seeds

Place the polenta and 1 litre cold water in a 2-litre saucepan. Cover, and bring to the boil. Once the water is boiling, reduce the heat and put a flame diffuser under the pan. Uncover the pan and simmer for 10–15 minutes, stirring from time to time, until the polenta softens. Switch off the heat and divide the polenta between 4 serving bowls. Add maple syrup to taste, and sprinkle with the sunflower seeds. Serve hot.

Creamy Polenta with Sunflower Seeds and Tofu Yoghurt

150g organic polenta
250 ml tofu yoghurt
50g sunflower seeds
sunflower oil

Place the polenta and 1 litre cold water in a 2-litre saucepan. Cover, and bring to the boil. Once the water is boiling, reduce the heat and put a flame diffuser under the pan. Uncover the pan and simmer for 10–15 minutes, stirring occasionally. Switch off the heat and divide the polenta between 4 serving bowls; top each bowl with a quarter of the tofu yoghurt.

To oil-roast the sunflower seeds you will need a heavy cast-iron frying pan. Add a few drops of sunflower oil, enough to coat the pan but so there is no oil 'swimming' in it, and spread it around with a pastry brush. Heat the pan for 1–2 minutes, then add the sunflower seeds. Roast, stirring occasionally for a few minutes, until the seeds are nice and brown but not burnt. Sprinkle on top of the yoghurt.

Polenta is a very popular staple in the Mediterranean. Made from ground corn kernels, it is not a whole grain as such, but it is still rich in nutrients.

Scrambled Tofu

1 tbsp sesame oil
1 small onion, coarsely grated
1 small carrot, coarsely grated
100g button mushrooms, finely sliced
500g organic tofu
1½ tbsp shoyu (or to taste)
½ tsp turmeric
steamed sourdough bread (see page 106)
organic natural mustard
2 small spring onions, finely chopped

Heat the oil in a medium-sized frying pan (cast-iron or stainless-steel) over a medium to high heat. Add the onion and carrot and stir for 1–2 minutes. Add the mushrooms and fry for a further 2 minutes. Crumble the tofu with your clean hands and add to the frying pan. Cook for 3–4 minutes until all the flavours mix in. Season with shoyu and turmeric, and cook for another minute. Turn off the heat and place the mixture in a serving dish. Serve with steamed sourdough bread spread with a thin layer of the mustard and sprinkled with the chopped spring onion.

Cous Cous and Oatflakes with Sunflower Seeds and Syrup

140g cous cous
50g porridge oats
1 tbsp tahini
1 medium orange, freshly squeezed
½ tsp sesame or sunflower oil
dry-roasted sunflower seeds, to decorate

Place the cous cous and oats in a 2-litre saucepan with 900ml cold water. Cover, and leave it to stand overnight. In the morning bring the cous cous and water to the boil, then uncover and simmer for 5 minutes on a low-medium heat. Add the tahini and cook for another 2–3 minutes. Turn off the heat and mix in the orange juice and oil. Sprinkle the sunflower seeds over the porridge to serve.

Pinhead Oat Porridge with Nori

180g pinhead oats
40g raisins
2 sheets of toasted nori, cut into 2-cm strips
2 tbsp toasted sesame seeds

Wash the oats and soak them overnight in 1 litre of cold water.

In the morning, bring the pinhead oats and the water to a boil in a 2-litre covered saucepan. Reduce the heat, uncover and simmer for 5 minutes. Add the raisins and cook for another 5 minutes, stirring occasionally to stop the ingredients from sticking to the bottom of the pan. Turn off the heat and leave to stand for 5 minutes. Serve with the strips of nori and sprinkled with the sesame seeds.

I like to mix pinhead barley with the oats: this makes the porridge deliciously creamy and crunchy at the same time. The proportions that work best are 150g pinhead oats and 30g pinhead barley.

Porridge is another one of those 'feed the five thousand' dishes. As a child I always ate oat flakes covered with sugar. Nowadays I replace the sugar with such delicacies as nori strips, sunflower or roasted pumpkin seeds, or even almonds. I don't think I could live in a world without porridge! When I'm run down I really crave it.

Terrific Teas

Terrific Teas

I was once famously quoted as saying I preferred a cup of tea to sex. Obviously, that is not true, although tea is a lot more available and less complicated! As a child, tea was a real mainstay: there was always a big green enamel tea pot chugging away on the stove, full of PG Tips. For our family, tea spelt hospitality. Interestingly, Drags says in Yugoslavia they only offered you tea if you were poorly, but in the English household one never needs an excuse for tea.

I found that one of the hardest things about turning macrobiotic was forgoing regular tea and coffee. I gave up coffee on the advice of a homeopathic doctor, and didn't touch it for six years. Then, while in Paris (how chic!), I relented and felt like I had taken class A drugs. I still sometimes pop in to those traditional coffee shops for a sniff because I love the smell of coffee, but drinking it makes me horribly hyper. I now love Bancha and Green Tea, but unlike Drags I have not managed to convert my family.

The majority of the teas in this chapter are medicinal and good for all sorts of common ailments. Bancha and Green Tea can be drunk on a regular basis but the

Strain Bancha Tea before you serve to avoid a mouthful of twigs

other teas should be more occasional. Bancha Tea is very low in tannin and extremely alkaline and refreshing. I always travel with a stash. Dried Daikon Tea is great for ridding the body of animal fats and is also very calming. Organic black soy beans, which are a nightmare to get hold of but worth the effort, can be made into a tea which is brilliant for strengthening the respiratory system. I've often used this tea on tour for tiredness in that area and it works a treat. Equally useful on tour, for those occasional champagne bashes, is the Umeboshi Bancha Tea, which Drags recommends for hangovers. Having this drink before you party can be preventative – but that's not an invitation to go ahead and abuse alcohol!

Because all of the teas featured in this chapter are low in caffeine, you can enjoy a cup at any time of the day, not just in the morning.

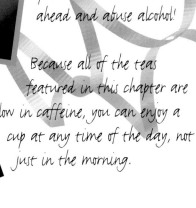

Shiitake Tea

**2 medium-sized dried shiitake
mushrooms**
¼ tsp shoyu

Soak the mushrooms in 200ml cold water until soft (this should take 10–15 minutes). Cut off and discard the stems and slice the caps. Put the mushrooms and 450ml water (including the soaking water) into a saucepan. Cover and bring to the boil. Reduce the heat to medium-low and simmer for 5 minutes. Add the shoyu and turn off the heat. Leave to stand for a couple of minutes, then strain and serve.

This tea is said to be good for reducing cholesterol levels in the blood and for detoxifying. In the East, shiitake mushrooms are known as anti-aphrodisiac, so steady on, especially if you use them in the fresh form.

Dried Daikon Tea

5g dried daikon

Place 1200ml water in a pan and add the dried daikon. Cover the pan and bring to the boil. Reduce the heat to medium-low and simmer for 10 minutes. Strain and serve.

It is a good idea to make enough tea for 3–4 servings and have 1 cup a day. Refrigerate any leftover tea and reheat it before drinking.

This tea is perfect if you need to relax. It also helps to rid the body of saturated fats.

Green and Brown Rice Tea

Boil 1200ml water, stand for 2 minutes. Put the tea leaves and roasted rice in a teapot and pour the water over them. Stand for a few minutes before serving. The water needs to be hot to produce the desired taste and the lovely light colour of the green tea.

Green tea is naturally grown tea. Unlike black tea it is not fermented. It contains some vitamins and minerals and is said to be helpful for reducing cholesterol. This particular mixture is very good for people who find the taste of pure green tea too strong or bitter. It comes in a packet under the name of 'mitsui genmai cha'.

4 tsp green and brown rice tea mixture

Sweet Kuzu

Put 300ml water into a small saucepan and place over a low heat. In a cup, dissolve the kuzu in a small amount of cold water. Add it to the cooking water and keep stirring constantly (to prevent lumps) until the water thickens (this should take only a few minutes). Put the rice syrup or barley malt in a cup and pour the hot kuzu over. Stir and drink warm.

This is a very relaxing drink. It is good for satisfying sweet cravings although it tastes nothing like a bar of chocolate!

1 tbsp kuzu
1 tsp brown rice syrup or barley malt

Kuzu is a very strong, wild, mountain root vegetable. The wild variety grows around and between rocks.

Bancha Twig Tea

1 tbsp bancha twigs

Place the twigs and 1 litre water in a saucepan. Bring to the boil then turn off. Leave for several minutes and serve.

Bancha twig tea has less caffeine than tea from tea leaves. It is very alkaline, and therefore good for any digestive problems caused by too much acid. It is also very good for babies who are teething (put your finger in a cup of warm tea and then rub it onto the baby's gums).

Shoyu Bancha with Spring Onion Drink

bancha twig tea (see above)
1 tsp shoyu
1 small spring onion, very finely chopped diagonally

Place the shoyu and spring onion in a cup. Pour the hot bancha twig tea over. Drink as hot as possible.

If you think you are getting a cold or flu it is best to drink this tea as hot as possible. Wrap up, get into bed, drink the tea and ideally you will sweat during the night. This should increase your resistance to infection.

Umeboshi Bancha Tea

bancha twig tea (see above)
¼–½ umeboshi (depends on the size, which varies)
½ tsp shoyu

Put the umeboshi and then the shoyu in a cup. Pour over the hot bancha tea and drink while warm.

This drink is good for digestive troubles, hangovers (tested on a few occasions!) and fatigue.

If you like Bancha Twig Tea, it is worth dedicating a kettle to the tea, because you can re-use the twigs (George and I both have a kettle just for bancha tea). Every time you make fresh tea, add half a teaspoon of fresh twigs and some more water. After 2–4 days, discard all the twigs and start afresh. I feed my plants with discarded bancha twigs.

Sweet Vegetable Tea

50g onions, cut into half moons
50g carrots, cut into matchsticks
50g cabbage, shredded
50g parsnips, cut into matchsticks

Bring 1750ml water to the boil, then lower the heat and add all the vegetables. Simmer for 15–20 minutes, covered. Strain and drink one cup while hot. Let the remaining tea cool down before storing it in the refrigerator. Each time you have a cup of this tea, warm up one serving in a pot to room temperature.

This is good if you have sweet cravings or need to relax.
To experience real benefit, have a cup a day for a month.

Agar Agar Drink

600ml sugar-free organic
apple juice
sea salt
1 tbsp agar agar

Combine the juice, a pinch of sea salt and the agar agar in a small saucepan. Cover and bring to the boil. Reduce the heat to medium-low and simmer for 10 minutes. Drink hot.

Although, unlike other sea vegetables, agar agar does not contain many nutrients, it is very helpful in cases of acute or even chronic constipation.

Parsley Tea

100g parsley, finely chopped

Place the parsley and 300ml water in a small saucepan. Cover and bring to the boil. Reduce the heat to medium-low and simmer for 5 minutes. Strain and serve.

Parsley tea is mostly used to help congested lungs. Drink one or two cups for two to three days to benefit. This tea is also generally refreshing, uplifting and energising.

Aduki Bean Tea

Put the beans, kombu and 1500ml water into a saucepan, cover and bring to the boil. Reduce the heat to very low and simmer, covered, for about 30 minutes. Strain and drink.

**50g aduki beans
3-cm piece kombu**

You may like to make enough tea for a few days, keep it refrigerated and use one cup at a time slightly warmed up. Keep the beans and use them in food dishes (such as soups, stews and casseroles). Make sure you cook them further until they are soft and edible.

Aduki beans, and particularly aduki bean tea, are said to be good for kidney and urinary troubles. On a few occasions I have recommended the tea to my friends who suffered from cystitis, and it worked. But some people find the taste of this tea overpowering.

Black Soy Bean Tea

Put the beans, kombu and 1500ml water together in a covered saucepan and bring to the boil. Reduce the heat and simmer on a medium-low heat for about 30–40 minutes. Strain and drink while warm. Save the beans to use in other dishes.

**50g organic black soy beans,
washed and rinsed
4–5-cm piece kombu**

This tea is said to be good for relieving coughing and generally for the respiratory organs. George likes to have some around the time when he performs. He swears by it, so check it out.

Glossary

A

aduki beans These small, dried red beans are also known as azuki beans.

agar agar See kanten

amasake A natural sweetener made from cooked sweet brown rice that comes in jars as a thick liquid. Millet and oat amasake are also available, but rice is always one of the ingredients.

arame This mild, brown sea vegetable comes in thin, dried strips that expand on soaking or cooking.

bancha twig tea This green tea, made from the twigs of mature Japanese tea bushes, is consumed in great quantities in Japan. It is available from good health food stores.

B

barley bread Excellent for those who are allergic to gluten, this is made out of barley flour instead of wheat flour.

barley malt (or barley syrup) A sweetener made by fermenting the starch in barley. Use in desserts and sweet sauces instead of sugar and honey.

brown rice syrup A natural sweetener made from rice, water and malted barley. Because it consists of polysaccharides, it helps to keep your blood glucose levels much steadier than sugar, which is made from monosaccharides.

brown rice vinegar This is a mild Japanese seasoning, ideal in dipping sauces. Choose organic versions.

burdock (also known as gobo) This long, slender dark brown root has an earthy aroma and crunchy texture and is delicious in stews, soups and vegetable dishes. The skin is full of flavour, so wash rather than peeling it. Submerge in cold water after cutting it to avoid discolouration.

C

Chinese cabbage A large, cylindrical greenish-white cabbage, widely available in supermarkets. Add to soups, stir-fries, salads and light stews. Delicious pickled, too.

corn and rice syrup A natural sweetener made from corn, water and malted brown rice.

D

daikon (also known as mooli) This long white radish is available in many supermarkets today.

G

ginger This root vegetable is available fresh, dried, pickled or ground. Fresh ginger imparts the richest taste; keep it in a cool, dry place. If you don't like the strong taste of whole pieces of ginger, you can grate it instead and just squeeze the juice into your dish, discarding the actual ginger. Pickled ginger has a very fresh taste, delicious with sushi and sashimi as it cleanses the palate between mouthfuls.

green and brown rice tea This mixture of green leaves and roasted brown rice is also known as mitsui genmai cha and is available from Japanese and Eastern food stores.

J

Japanese seven spice See shichimi

K

kanten A vegetable setting agent similar to gelatin. It is made by drying and freezing extracts of various sea vegetables. It is also known as agar agar and is available in flakes.

kombu (konbu or kelp) This seaweed generally comes dried in packets, of varying grades of quality. It is traditionally used in Japan with bonito flakes to make dashi, a type of stock. Don't wash kombu or its flavour will leach out.

kuzu powder An effective thickener, available from Japanese and health food shops in a lumpy looking white powder. It dissolves easily in water to make a glossy, translucent thickening agent for soups, sauces, desserts and stews. It is also used to make tea.

L

lemon grass A long, fibrous pale green-white stalk, usually ground to a paste with other ingredients or shredded as a flavouring for soups.

M

mirin This sweet rice cooking wine is delicious in sauces, stir-fries and sautés.

miso A protein-rich, soybean paste, available in a whole variety of colours, textures and flavours. It generally comes in jars or heavy-duty plastic bags. Yellow (shinshu) miso is a quick fermented type. White (shiro) miso is sweet, excellent in dressings. Barley (mugi) miso is dark brown and earthy in flavour. Hatcho miso is aged, dark brown, and good in soups.

mochi A glutinous rice cake, generally available in packaged squares or sheets. Delicious for breakfast.

N

nori (also known as laver) Most commonly used to wrap sushi rolls, this dark green-brown seaweed is sold in dried sheet form. You can toast it yourself or buy it ready toasted.

P

pak choy (also referred to as bok choy) This is a leafy green vegetable ideal for soups, stews and stir-fries. Avoid over-cooking it as it will lose its crunchy texture as well as its vitamins and minerals.

pinhead oats A coarse type of oatmeal.

polenta Made from cornmeal, this is a staple in many Mediterranean countries. Most supermarkets stock it.

pumpkin seeds Rich in calcium and protein, these are available dried from most supermarkets or health food stores.

R

rice This comes in many forms: short grain, brown, sweet brown, sticky, sushi. Sweet brown rice is very glutinous.

rice milk Ideal with desserts or on cereal, this is a non-dairy alternative to milk.

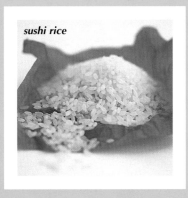

sushi rice

S

sake Japanese rice wine, used in cooking but also a very popular drink. Available from all Japanese stores, you can drink it hot or cold.

seitan A wheat protein made from flour and water, cooked with ginger, shoyu and kombu.

sesame oil This has a wonderful, rich flavour and is one of the essential ingredients in macrobiotic cooking. Always use organic, cold-pressed oil. The toasted variety has a nuttier taste than the standard one.

sesame seeds Sesame seeds are a rich source of calcium, protein and iron. They come in two colours: brown and black. We usually prefer to use black ones, which have the richest taste.

shichimi A combination of seven dried and ground spices – good for sprinkling over noodle dishes or bean and grain soups. It comes in small jars which should be kept tightly shut to lock in the aroma.

shiitake mushrooms You can buy these fresh or dried. Fresh shiitake have a delicate and slightly woody taste. The dried variety need to be soaked to reconstitute them before cooking: use the flavoursome soaking liquid in your dish. The stems of dried shiitake are usually too tough to eat, however, so discard before cooking.

shoyu (also known as soy sauce) A pungent, salty brown sauce made from soybeans, wheat and salt. It comes in 'light' and 'dark' varieties.

wakame

soba (buckwheat) noodles Thin, grey-brown noodles, available dried in packets.

sourdough bread Cooked without yeast, it can be made from most grains, but the most common ones are rice, rye and barley. It is particularly good for people who are allergic to wheat.

soy cream A great non-dairy alternative to cream: good for sweet and savoury dishes. Comes in cartons.

soy dessert This non-dairy custard is available in two flavours: vanilla and chocolate.

T
tahini A sesame seed paste available in jars. It makes good sauces, dips and dressings.

tofu This soy bean curd comes dried or fresh (which can be soft, firm, extra firm or smoked). For fresh tofu, we like to use the Full of Beans or Clear Spot brands, available from health food or Japanese stores; store fresh tofu, covered in water, in the fridge. Dried tofu should be reconstituted in hot water before cooking.

U
udon noodles Round or flat, white noodles made from wheat.

umeboshi A Japanese plum which is pickled when green and unripe and turns red thanks to the preserving process. The plums are very strong, so use sparingly. A paste is also available in jars.

umeboshi vinegar Made from the liquid in which umeboshi plums are pickled. It has a slightly fruity flavour.

W
wakame This edible sea vegetable is rich in minerals and proteins. It looks similar to kombu but is softer. A small amount goes a long way. You can find it in dried form in most health food stores; but you may also find it fresh, too.

wasabi A Japanese horseradish, pale green in colour and more aromatic and mild than its Western counterpart. It comes in powder form or ready made up in a tube. I prefer to use the powder, as it is free of preservatives.

Y
yannoh coffee This instant 'coffee' mixture is made from barley, rye, malted barley, chicory and acorns. It makes an excellent caffeine-free alternative to coffee.

Index

Acknowledgements

My thanks to:
My dad for bringing home the bacon and my mum for cooking it. Drags for endless nourishment, and Simon. Jelena for her seitan. Eileen for buying me fish and chips. Paul and Ray for being such good food couriers. Darren Evans for making me look flawless. Siobhan for washing up. Kim Andreolli for covering me in noodles. Toni Gordon and Yvonne at 'Wedge'. Jamie Gidlow-Jackson for simmering my emotions. And food for being a loyal friend and a love substitute.

Boy George

My thanks to:
All at C&B, I hope you haven't missed many meals working on this book. To the farmers and those who bring food to us. Mother for the nourishment. Patsy, mum-in-law, for that extra nourishment. Jelena, I love you. My Yugo chums Ljilja, Leo, Jimmy, Drita and Rads: HVALA. Karin, merci beaucoup. Krista, my favourite Yankee. Peter at 'Sesame', the no. 1 health food shop in Primrose Hill, London! Jeremy, for the sexist jokes. George, for loving me. Dusica and Enno veilen Dank for the unforgettable Klosters days. Mel for the best macro food I've eaten outside my home. Kim Andreolli, for the 'numero uno' photographs in the book. Milos, my bro, Ankica, Mica, Vlada and Maja. Takashi THANK YOU. Lorenzo, mille grazie bello. Bob Lloyd, for the best macro soups. Mosbachers for being my pals. Mr and Mrs Miura of 'Miyama' for the best Japanese restaurant in the world. Lucy Knox and Sarah for the fun shoots. Denny, the best macro councillor on the planet, thank you, thank you, thank you. Christopher, for the help, Alexander for the care, Nicholas for being a rascal, Michael for being special. Simon for substituting food for sex. No wonder I'm so thin!!!

Dragana G. Brown, www.chienergy.co.uk

Carroll & Brown would like to thank:
David Murray, Jules Selmes and Kim Andreolli for photography; Lizzie Harris for food styling; Jane Bamforth for editing the recipes; Charlotte Beech for editorial assistance; Evie Loizides for design assistance.

Front jacket: Kim Andreolli